RESC

RESONANCE

BIBLICAL TEXTS
SPEAKING TO
21ST CENTURY INQUIRERS

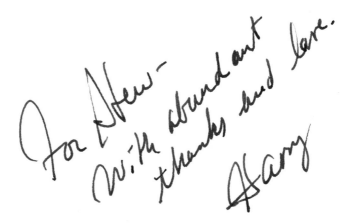

HARRY T. COOK

"Deep calleth unto deep in the thunder of thy cataracts."
—Psalm 42:7

POLEBRIDGE PRESS
Salem, Oregon

Cover and interior design by Robaire Ream

Library of Congress Cataloging-in-Publication Data
Cook, Harry T., 1939-
  Resonance : Biblical texts speaking to 21st century inquirers / Harry T. Cook.
    p. cm.
  ISBN 978-1-59815-029-2 (alk. paper)
 1. Bible--Criticism, interpretation, etc. 2. Bible. N.T. Gospels--Criticism, interpretation, etc. I. Title.
  BS511.3.C658 2011
  226'.06--dc22
                              2011002160

For

Susan
Robert and Elizabeth
Martin and Christine
Sarah and Robert
Max
Alyssa, Cameron, Grace and Julien

μείξων δὲ τούτων ἡ ἀγάπη

TABLE OF CONTENTS

PREFACE

It could only have been for the convenience of easier reading that Johannes Gutenberg printed the Bible in book form, having cast its contents as he found them in uniform type and arranging the type in neat columns. Any such book invites the reader to start at page one and read through to the end. Yet neither the Bible nor this book is meant to be read in that fashion.

The Bible is a collection of documents, in some cases fragments of documents, cobbled together over a period of as many as a thousand years spanning several epochs, including the Babylonian, the Persian, the Mesopotamian, and the Graeco-Roman along with their various subcultures. With the exception of a few Aramaic words and Aramaisms, the biblical documents appear in Hebrew and Koiné Greek with many remnants from other ancient tongues lurking here and there.

Anyone who tells you that he or she has "read the Bible from cover to cover" is probably lying or at the very least uninformed as to its nature. One does not go into a public library and start with auto mechanics and work his way through to zoology. One goes to a library seeking a volume of fiction or biography or history—or even an auto mechanics manual.

The word "bible" entered the English language from the German "bibliothek," meaning library. And like the anthology commonly known by that title, this book is a small "library" of analytical essays, accompanied by translations and paraphrases, of 24 familiar and, in the author's

1

judgment, important biblical texts—arranged in chapter form with appropriate titles. It is suggested that the reader treat this book as a "library," scanning the Table of Contents for titles and accompanying texts that meet particular needs at particular times.

It should be understood that the author is honing no blade of theological or ideological agenda in these analyses. He has treated the texts much as an archaeologist treats shards from a dig, examining them closely and in reference to their context with no preconceived notion of how each might fit into a completed whole, should it ever be possible or desirable to construct one.

Altered versions of several of the essays have appeared in an ongoing series the author has been publishing online for several years. The series called Findings II is a successor to Findings, published in 2003 by the Church Publishing Group—a subsidiary of the (Episcopal) Church Pension Fund. It is known that homilists across the United States and Canada, as well as in Great Britain and Australia, have read, marked, learned, and inwardly digested the material presented in the online series and have used its contents not only in sermon preparation but for the education of the laity.

The passages treated herein have been translated by the author and then paraphrased with two concerns in mind: a) how ordinary people of first-century CE Palestine may have read or, more probably, heard them and b) how twenty-first-century English speakers in the western world can best appropriate them for instruction, inspiration, and understanding. English renditions of New Testament Greek words appear in the author's own idiosyncratic transliterations fashioned to help readers unfamiliar with Koiné Greek pronounce them and thus to "hear" them as they may have been heard in the time they were put down. On occasion, the actual Greek is used.

The format is three-fold: 1) the translation and para-phrase, 2) a section called Workshop in which the exegesis and analysis appear, and 3) a final section called Homiletic Commentary, an expository treatment of the text to aid those who would prepare sermons on the text or lead groups studying the text. Together the three sections are intended to help readers who may have limited resources at hand deal in some depth with the biblical material.

When one is trying to wrest some measure of relevance and contemporaneity from the texts, it is important to be reminded that authors whose identities are long since lost in the tangle of history were clearly deep thinkers who, in amazingly different literary styles, told stories, created parables, wrote songs, and otherwise commented upon their times. They left a trove of literature that still invites scholar, dilettante, and casual reader alike into circumstances the lineaments of which can barely be surmised at this remove.

Yet since their evolution into what anthropologists call "modern man," human beings have loved and hated, hoped and despaired, relished and rued in pretty much the same ways. That is why we can read the *Iliad* today and feel for Achilles and Hector what Homer imagined they might have endured some 3,000 and more years ago. The same applies to other such myth-enshrouded figures as Abraham, Isaac, Jacob, Moses, Ruth, Saul, David, Uriah, Bathsheba, and the various literary characters to be found in the pages of the New Testament.

One of my working hypotheses is that the New Testament documents, one and all, belong to the category of political and religious history and, in particular, to church history. Setting aside the unhelpful and entirely unsupportable assertion that biblical literature is exempt from the ordinary rigors of objective investigation because it is somehow sacred, I have worked at my textual analyses following the canons of academic research, going where the data lead rather than forcing the data to lead me to places a religious tradition or its hierarchy would have me led.

Finally, it is a happy duty to acknowledge those who have helped me over the years, including Charles Kessler, who taught me Hebrew and Greek; Helmer Ringgren, who introduced me to Akkadian and taught me Aramaic and advanced Hebrew; and the late George Arthur Buttrick, himself a scholar and master preacher, who was my homiletics professor and from whom I learned a great deal about the Greek New Testament. Those who read this book should know of Tom Hall, my most excellent editor, who saved them from many a complex sentence put down by a writer who never saw a subordinate clause he didn't like. The patient people of St. Andrew's Episcopal Church in Clawson, Michigan, who had the dubious advantage of having a working scholar for a rector over two decades, must also be acknowledged. Those dear people could not sit through a Sunday homily all those years without some Aramaic, Hebrew or Greek term being cast in their teeth along with Cook's English rendering of it in an attempt to demonstrate its alleged relevance to them. They were the guinea pigs for this experiment and were the first to hear much of what follows in these pages.

—Harry T. Cook
August 31, 2010

MANDATE FOR COMMUNITY

John 13:30–35

After Judas received his piece of bread, he left. It was night. After that, Jesus said, "Now you will see the reputation of the One like us in all its glory in which you will see what God is like. God has been honored in the reputation of the One like us, and that you will see very soon. Dear ones, I won't be with you very much longer. You will look for me, but as I said to the Jews I am also saying to you now: 'Where I am going, you cannot come.' Meanwhile, I give you a new mandate: 'Love one another as I have loved you. In the same way that I have given myself to you, give yourselves to each other. This is how people will know that you are my followers, if you have that kind of love for each other."

Rubric

"Remember that Thanksgiving when we were all around the table together. It was the last time before Dad died. Remember what he said?" So go human memories of "last times" and of their impact. That is the sense of the passage above. Its writer knew the end of the story before he wrote the first word of its beginning. He wrote it for a community or communities whose members were trying to remember things they may never have known in the first place. By the time the Gospel according to John made its appearance, as many as six decades had passed since whatever events took place became stylized in their retelling as the Passion of Jesus Christ.

5

It is not coincidental that the event depicted in the passage above took place as a community had sat down to eat, in this case a meal that had some significance beyond itself having to do with the Jewish Passover. That's how it often works. A family gathers periodically for a kind of *über* meal and uses the occasion to call to mind its collective past. They eat together because they love one another or at least try to do so because that's how families behave at their best, especially when, softened by sentiment and nostalgia, they are remembering earlier times.

Workshop

So the reading begins: "At the last supper when Judas had gone out, Jesus said . . ." And he said it at length. The discourse begins at 13:31 and goes on from there with few interruptions and stage directions through to 17:26 just prior to John's depiction of the handing over (or turning in) of Jesus by Judas Iscariot. This is what might be called the end of the beginning, if not the beginning of the end. The memorable "love" enunciated at 13:34–35 certainly resonates with the later, post-resurrection "forgiveness" theme of John 20:22–23 ("If you forgive the sins of any, they are forgiven . . .").

John may not have been the obvious dramatist that Luke was, but the first words of the text at hand are drama enough: "After receiving the piece of bread, Judas immediately went out. And it was night." John was not telling us what time it was. Darkness in this drama is descending and will not be lifted until Mary Magdalene is depicted as recognizing the risen Jesus at the tomb (John 20:16ff). Speaking of drama, John accomplished the betrayer's exit (13:31a) only to make way for a triumphal speech from the soon-to-be-betrayed to the effect that the mischief Judas had gone on his way to make would "glorify" both the Son of Man (or One like us) the Father who is in him.

John's Christology is sufficiently formed that he can put on Jesus' lips the words, "No one has greater love than this, to lay down one's life for his friends" (15:13). That statement can be taken in a political-historical context, meaning that Jesus took the bullet for a whole community of dissidents Rome no doubt wanted out of its hair, or in a metaphysical context meaning that Jesus' death would be atonement for human sin. Taken together with John 3:16, 15:13 could mean the latter. But considered with the word "friends" in mind, it could yet mean the former. In any event, John was saying that sacrificial love is the divine nature disclosed by and in the Son

That established, John's Jesus got down to the application of the principle: "Little children," he said (John representing it in the Greek "teknia," which is almost akin to "kids" or, better, "dear ones"), "Yet a little while I am with you." This is notice that a) Jesus wasn't long for this world because they were coming to get him and silence him, or b) that his life as an incarnated terrestrial was coming to an end. As he told "the Jews" (see 7:33, 8:21 and 13:33), "Where I am coming you cannot come"—and that could mean a) that his would be a singular martyrdom or b) that his ultimate destination was re-absorption into the Godhead whence he had been incarnated. A good many Johannine passages are double-entendres. Either way, Jesus was depicted as leaving behind a community that he created, and it is obvious that the community will have a continuing vocation beyond its relationship to him. This is its singular vocation: "A new mandate" to love one another as he has loved it/them.

Homiletic Commentary

It is the "newness" factor that is the low-hanging homiletic fruit of this passage. This "new commandment"—what is "new" about it? The "love" commandment is otherwise stated as "to love the other as self"—a riff on Hillel.[1] But what is "new" here is that love is to be expressed as Jesus is depicted as having expressed it, viz., in a full, self-giving, sacrificial way. Here are echoes of the Qumran brotherly love concept of the sons (and presumably the daughters) "of light" loving one another. It is not, though, a necessarily universal, undiscriminating love that is enjoined here, but a ratcheting up of fraternal love (φιλέω) to all-out, no-holds-barred love (αγάπη).

Already one supposes that anyone who had shared Jesus' itinerancy, as the disciples are depicted as having done, would have had and expressed some measure of fraternal love for one another. Now comes the higher vocation: to love one another as Jesus is said to have loved them. And the exhortation has a specific purpose: "This is how people will know that you are my followers, if you have that kind of love for each other." So αγάπη (agapā) has both intrinsic and extrinsic values. It is how a community lives when this is its primary teaching—which may explain why much of the world regards institutional Christianity as a joke. The contemporary Anglican Communion, for example, has strayed far from what the only proper noun in this sentence supposedly conveys. It is a cat-fight on a global scale. It is that, too, in its United States province, the Episcopal Church.

The Episcopal Church has clawed and scratched its way along, fighting such intramural battles as slavery: the church in the American South pretty much stuck with the Confederacy. The church came close to schism in its General Convention's decision to divert church funds to the American inner cities that had been ravaged by revolts in the mid-sixties. Then came the unseemly conflict over altering liturgical language, followed closely by its schism-baiting debate over whether or not women could be priests and bishops. Now the abyss widens over whether gay and lesbian persons are human enough to be anything other than barely tolerated sinners.

Add to that the confusion into which the Roman Catholic Church has fallen with its hierarchy's systematic attempt to fend off criticism of its failure for who knows how long to discipline its pedophile priests. Treating the Vatican as if it were an impregnable fortress that no one dare storm and of whose colonels and generals no journalist dare ask pointed questions, the pope and his acolytes wrap themselves in the vestments of faux piety and sneer back at the world they say their Lord was sent to save.

"They will know we are Christians by our love, by our love. They will know that we are Christians by our love."[2] So go the words to a song made popular during the post-Vatican II adjustments in American Catholicism.

I think the world knows no such thing.

Notes

1. Hillel the Elder was a famous Jewish religious teacher who lived in Jerusalem during the time of King Herod around the beginning of the Common Era. Among his best-known teachings is: "That which is hateful to you, do not do to your fellow. That is the whole Torah; the rest is the explanation. Now go and learn" (Talmud: Shabbat 31a).

2. Peter Scholtes and Carolyn Arends, © 1966 by F.E.L. Publications, Ltd./ASCAP.

LOVE DESPITE IT ALL

Luke 15:11ff

A man had two sons, and the older of them said, "Father, give me the share of the property that will be mine after you die." So the father apportioned his property between the two. Shortly thereafter the younger son converted his share to cash and went to a distant country where he ended up, as it were, sowing his seed and living as if there were no tomorrow. When all his money was gone it happened that a severe depression hit the country and people were hungry. He found himself in need and got himself hired by a Gentile to feed his pigs. He thought someone would give him food for his work, but ended up thinking the slop he had to feed the pigs was beginning to look good. When he couldn't take it any longer, he thought better of his choices and remembered that his father's hired help were fed decent food for their trouble while he, a son, was dying of hunger. So he decided to swallow his pride and go home. He concocted a speech he hoped would win a favorable reception: "Father, I have done wrong to you and to God, and I am no longer worth to be considered your son. So take me on as a hired hand." Thus prepared, he started for home. When he drew near to home, his father saw him coming at some distance. His father's gut reaction was to forgive, so he ran down the road to meet his son. The father embraced the son and kissed him. The son started his speech of contrition but was

10

interrupted by the father's order to his servants to bring the garb of a son, not a field hand: a costly robe, a ring, and sandals for his feet—and not only that, but to prepare a huge welcome-home celebration, because the father had thought his son was as good as dead. Meanwhile the older son was at his accustomed work in the field and wondered what all the fuss was. When told, he grew angry and refused to join the party. His father came out and begged him to come in, but the older son balked, saying, "All these years I have worked for you and never disobeyed you and you have never celebrated that. Now this good-for-nothing son of yours turns up—the one who took your gift and threw it away in payments to prostitutes, and now you butcher a calf for him?" The father replied, "Son, you are always with me, and all I have is yours. But we had to have this celebration because your brother was dead and has come back to life. He was lost and is found."

Rubric

You may as well ask whether the great fish swallowed and subsequently spat out Jonah as to ask if the story of the prodigal son is the report of an actual series of events. Of course it is not. Yet the truth it conveys about family relationships, the difference in character among human beings, and the evangelist's surmise of divine-human relationships can hardly be denied.

This so-called "parable of the prodigal son" certainly ranks in the Christian world with the 23d Psalm, 1 Corinthians 13, and the Lord's Prayer for cherished religious texts. One wants very much to think that someone named Jesus— "the" Jesus to more orthodox believers—told this story pretty much as it appears in Luke 15. If "a" or "the" Jesus did not tell the story or one very much like it, the parable's sentiment nonetheless fits well with the ethic of one of the prominent sayings attributed to a Jesus: "Forgive seventy times seven" (Matthew 18:21, var. Luke 17:4).

To believe with any intellectual honesty that "the" Jesus told the prodigal's story, one would have to posit for it (as some analyst have done) an early and original source that only Luke would have known about and/or that only Luke used. If it were not original with Luke or some proto-Lukan tradition, surely some other gospel writer would have included it in some form. Yet the story appears only in Luke.

Of course, neither the prodigal son story nor its theme of unconditional forgiveness fits too well with Matthew 25:31–46, wherein judgment of the goats, certainly not forgiveness, is paramount. Nor is it likely that many followers of first-century CE Jesus Judaism, not to mention emerging synagogue Judaism, would have been ready for the universalism suggested by Luke in the parable.

Workshop

A good many exegetes have turned themselves into eisegetes[1] in their efforts to parse this parable, and thus have treated it as an allegory. Called "the parable of the prodigal son" by translators of the English bible of the late 1500s, its central figure is certainly the father. And while the dispositions and actions of both younger and elder sons are the color and melodrama of the piece, it is the father's disposition and action that make the story what it is and define its parabolic point—namely, that the father's love for both his sons extends to understanding and forgiving the younger's rejections of him and the elder's rejection of the younger.

One can make a case that the original parable (whether from the lips of "a" or "the" Jesus) comprises vv. 1–24 while 25–32 constitute a kind of midrash added later. There is much to commend such a hypothesis, inasmuch as 15:24 reads like a dramatic ending—"'This son of mine was dead and is alive; he was lost and is found!' And they began to celebrate"—an ending that constitutes the father's uncompromising explanation for the feast.

If as I have long proposed, the gospels are in large part the history of nascent Christianity, the second part of the parable featuring the resentment of the older son may have been added to take into account the rift between the more or less established communities of Jesus Judaism and Gentile converts—the figure of the elder son being a sympathetic contact point for Jews who may have felt ill used by the ready acceptance of uninitiated Gentile converts. Think here of the conflict depicted between Gentile and Jewish identity depicted in Acts 15:1–29 and Galatians 2:1–21, and of the mediating role assigned by Luke to James in Acts 15:13–21.

Rudolf Bultmann and others insist that that the entirety of Luke 15:11–32 is of a piece and in more or less its original form (whatever they mean by "original"), and that the two distinct sections of the parable are necessary to the main point of the whole—namely, that divine forgiveness embraces both the egregious and blasphemous wastrel and the faithful but intolerant good brother.

It is worth noting that Luke has the younger son ask for his patrimony as if his father were already dead. Since he was chronologically the second of two sons, the older would, by custom of the time and place, get two-thirds of the estate and he himself one third. Luke says the father "divided" the substance between them, meaning perhaps that Luke for theological purposes wanted to depict the abused father as being even more generous than custom provided. In any event, it appears that in Luke's imagination the father held on to much of his wealth by means of what we today would call "life estate" in order to continue the home-front enterprise and to be able (and ready, as it turns out) to lay on a big feast upon the prodigal's return.

Also to be noted is that in Luke's imagination, "When he came to himself"—i.e., when sobriety and common sense returned—the prodigal began to calculate the cost of his stupidity and resultant loss, and composed a speech to give to his father on whose mercy he was about to throw himself. Yet he can't even get to the front door before his father meets him on the road, and leads him back into the bosom of his family. The point is that he was *nekros*—dead—and now, the joyous father proclaims, is alive. The death may refer to the custom of the time according to which a son who treated a father as the prodigal did was as good as dead, cut off not necessarily by the family but by the exercise of his own poor choice.

A parable by its very nature invites one to identify with its oft-told story and perhaps with one character or another, though maybe not the same one each time. Thus the story ends up meaning one thing to one person and another to the next, and to each a different thing at a different time.

Homiletic Commentary

My revered teacher, the late Dr. George A. Buttrick, said of this parable: "No story more instantly touches the nerve of actual life. Let it be read, without any comment or explanation, and it conquers us."[2] At ten, my daughter, now the very bright and analytical law school graduate, used to ask me to read her the parable at bedtime. I never asked why, but I knew it spoke to her in some way. The sentiment it engendered may have produced my Father's Day card from her one year. It was a photo of a father holding his daughter by the hand. The message read: "For listening any time, for believing every time, for loving me all the time. . . ."

As the world moves away from serious consideration of the old gods of the old religions, away from the lovely but impossible idea that an invisible deity holds all in its hands and will make everything all right somehow, what will become of such stories as the father and his prodigal son?

The father, as Luke depicted him, was the avatar of unconditional love, and, more than that, of an aggressive love. His love for his sons—the younger a terminally disrespectful wastrel, the elder an insufferable prig—was entirely independent of their conduct toward each other and toward him. That image must have hovered over the labors of the hymn writer as he paraphrased the 23rd Psalm thus: "Perverse and foolish oft I strayed, but yet in love he sought me, and on his shoulder gently laid, and home, rejoicing, brought me."[3]

Of course, both the psalmist and the hymnist were envisioning the biblical deity, the former no doubt in images evoked by some gentle shepherd of his acquaintance, the latter by the psalm itself and the "good shepherd" appellation associated with Jesus of Nazareth, especially by John the Evangelist (see John 10:11–18).

In any event, the parable makes the singular point that steadfast and unconditional love is lavished upon the prodigal after his return from the fleshpots. He had earned disgrace and opprobrium many times over, and any jury, save one composed of other rehabilitated prodigals, would have found him guilty and imposed the stiffest penalty.

How to regard this beloved text with intellectual honesty? Given the uncritical deference accorded the Bible, even by clergy who should know better, it will be a difficult proposition. Buttrick's suggestion that it be read without any comment or explanation is not a bad idea, but it would then have to be read as Richard Burton or Charles Laughton might have read it: movingly and memorably. Failing that, the story might be seen as a large-canvas painting best appreciated from a distance and regarding it both in its parts and as a whole. A homilist or teacher, like a knowing docent, might point out this shadow, that shaft of light, etc. He or she might ask the congregation to imagine sights, sounds and smells not accounted for in the story.

It would not be at all inappropriate to focus on Luke's remarkable father-figure and to ask how his demeanor, restraint, and generosity might be seen as models for a nation's foreign and domestic policy initiatives, or as the governing ideals of community organization, of civic virtue, of family life.

Notes

1. The term "eisegete" means one who puts into a text while "exegete" is one who digs out what's in it.

2. Buttrick, George A., *The Parables of Jesus* (Harper & Brothers, 1928), p. 189.

3. Henry Williams Baker, "The King of love my shepherd is" in *The Hymnal 1982* (New York: Church Hymnal Corp., c1985), p. 645.

KILLING THE MESSENGER TO SUPPRESS THE MESSAGE

Luke 4:16ff

When Jesus returned to Galilee, he came to Nazareth where he had grown up and on Shabbat joined the local assembly as had been his custom. He volunteered to read the Haftarah portion; an attendant gave him the Isaiah scroll and Jesus chose to read these words: "The Spirit of Adonoi is upon me because he has set me apart to bring good news to the poor. He has sent me to proclaim release to those held captive and recovery of sight to the blind, to lift the burden from the oppressed, and to proclaim a time of grace. . . . On this very day, the promise of this writing has been fulfilled in me while you sat there listening. . . . In very truth I tell you that no prophet is accepted as such in his own home town" . . . and they drove him out of town. . . .

Rubric

Except for extreme and unredeemable racists and for those who believe only confirmed members of their opposition party are fit to govern, the American nation rejoiced in the election of Barack Obama in November 2008, and two and a half months later in his inauguration as the 44th President of the United States. The celebration sometimes had a manic, over-the-top feeling about it. One almost thought for a moment of a conquering Caesar standing triumphantly in a chariot as the loyal troops marching behind him chanted a lusty song of victory.

A year later, a significant portion of the nation fell out of love with the one they believed might be a political messiah. "What is this? A new teaching—with authority," is what the congregation of the Nazarene synagogue had said of their hometown boy made good. "All spoke well of him," as the Gospel according to Mark says. Not much later they want to kill him. Why? Because: "No prophet is acceptable in the prophet's hometown." And why that? Because unless the prophet speaks smooth things, asks nothing, and gives everything at no cost to all those with their hands out, he is a dead man—or as good as dead.

Workshop

With a reprise of the "On this very day, the promise of this writing has been fulfilled in me while you sat there listening," Luke introduces the second act of the Nazarene drama. At first his fellow townspeople are welcoming of Jesus, won over and impressed by his familiar lineage (Joseph's son). Luke's Jesus dazzles his fellow Nazarenes until he reminds them that eventually the effect of his gifted oratory will fade and his prophetic message will be resented. Why does Luke have him make that assumption? Perhaps this begins Luke's carefully crafted process of rejection, the end of which will be depicted down the road as execution.

It is as if Luke's "They got up and drove him out of the town . . ." were the historical basis for ("He came to what was his own, and his own people did not accept him" John 1:11). For whatever reason, though, Luke has Jesus escape the wrath of the Nazarenes on that occasion.

How could that have been? Suppose for a moment that the Nazareth event actually occurred pretty much as Luke depicted it. Jesus would probably have gotten roughed up in some way. Suppose that on such an occasion he had actually been killed. His followers over time could have morphed such a local event into a national one, much as Paul transformed the eventual execution from a national event into one of universal import (see Colossians 1:15ff: "Christ Jesus is the image of the invisible God, the first born of all creation . . . all things have been created through him . . . he himself is before all things . . . and you who were once estranged and hostile in mind, doing evil deeds, he has now reconciled in his fleshly body through his death . . ."

The maxim first proposed by Mark about the prophet being without honor in his own territory is almost certainly borrowed from another, earlier source, and it reflects a common experience. The idea is that someone with whom you played sandlot baseball or hopscotch, and with whom from childhood you were on a first-name basis, and with whom you exchanged all those childhood secrets, is hardly a person of whose unsearchable wisdom you'd necessarily be convinced.

When Luke employed the maxim, it was probably meant to apply to all Israel under the term "hometown" just as John thus observed that the entire creation, which in John's view had sprung directly from the eternal logos of which Jesus himself was an incarnation, rejected him.

The rejection motif may reflect the thinking of early Jesus-movement groups as they strove to shape their societies around the ethical wisdom of their hero and at the same time felt it necessary to explain why Jesus at one point or another apparently died in the cause of that countercultural wisdom in which salvation is understood as having to do not with the just deserts of retributive justice in a then-and-there but with the fruits of distributive justice in the here-and-now—and, you might say, with the corrective of abuses inflicted on ordinary people by the principalities and powers. The gaming of the financial system by Wall

Street tycoons in the first decade of the 2000s comes to mind.

Homiletic Commentary

It might occur to the serious inquirer to ask how a given congregation or some larger community of organized Christian-oriented believers might avoid reacting to the gospel's necessary critique of society as the Nazarenes and others reacted—that is, by driving the messenger away.

The annals of clergy deployment are overstuffed with narratives about men and women who came to understand that the gospel was radically egalitarian, even socialistic, and went on to so inform the congregations who had employed and subsequently fired them. If the "hometown" of the gospel passage at hand stands for the parish to which a clergy person has accepted appointment, it is often enough the case that, like the utterances of the prophets alluded to in the maxim, the sermons of said clergy person advocating gospel-based social action go unhonored, to put it mildly.

In the weeks and months following the revolt of African Americans in Detroit now more than 40 years ago, the rector whom I served as curate told his congregation that all the fuss about the then-current issue of open housing was nothing with which Christians needed to be concerned. He said, in effect, that it didn't matter if "the blacks" were purposely zoned out of certain areas by real estate covenants "because there is open housing in heaven."

For that piece of theological idiocy he was much praised by many. The following Sunday was my turn in the pulpit, and I could not resist unsaying what he had said. I tried my best to sweeten the medicine, but I could not spare him the dose.

I told the congregation that "heaven" should be understood as a biblical metaphor for what life here and now was envisioned by Jesus and other wisdom teachers to be, namely a society of people committed to live according to such ethical principles as the Golden Rule. Therefore, anyone who claims the privilege of living where he or she wishes must not lay so much as a straw in the way of any other who wishes to claim it, too.

One of the leading lay persons of that congregation told me after church that I knew where I could stick my "therefore." My boss wasted little time in getting me off the payroll and out of his hair. That would not be the last time I would be considered persona non grata for such an offense as reporting what the gospel obviously said and applying it to current events. We had, among other things yet to come, the Vietnam war, draft resistance, the battle for reproductive rights, the curse of the Moral Majority, and Reaganomics.

IT LOOKS CUTE, BUT
IF ONE TAKES IT
SERIOUSLY . . .

Luke 3:15–17, 21–22

John the Baptist had gotten people all excited and they were wondering if he might be the Messiah. But he told them, "I baptize you with water; but one who has more power than I do is coming; I am not worthy to so much as untie his shoes. He will baptize you with the Holy Spirit and fire. His pitchfork is in his hand to clear the threshing floor and to gather the wheat into his granary; but the chaff he will burn with a fire you will be unable to put out." . . . Now when John had baptized all who came, and when Jesus himself had been baptized and was off praying, the Holy Spirit came down on him in the form of a dove. And a voice was heard from somewhere up above, saying, "You are my Son, the beloved one; with you I am very pleased."

Rubric

Imagine being an intelligent extra-terrestrial dropping into a Christian church during the rite of baptism and wondering what the man or woman in the long white robe was supposed to be doing to a baby by pouring water over its head. You would probably conclude that you were witnessing an antique ritual intended to wash away the evil spirits or some such thing. In a way, you would be right. Being of superior intelligence, you would know that an ounce or two of tepid water would not avail for any true cleansing. You would know further that the infant being so washed would experience probable, albeit minor, discomfort. You would likely wonder at the furtive snapping of cameras and the oohing and aahing of grown-up people witnessing the event.

Depending on what kind of church you were visiting, the answers to your question of what's going on here and why? could range widely. You might be told it was "A death unto sin, and a new birth unto righteousness: for being by nature born in sin, and the children of wrath, we are hereby made the children on grace."[1] Or someone might say, "Infants are baptized so that they can share citizenship in the Covenant, membership in Christ, and redemption by God."[2] Another might insist that "Baptism is a Sacrament which cleanses us from original sin, makes us Christians, children of God, and heirs of heaven. Actual sins and all the punishment due to them are remitted by Baptism, if the person baptized be guilty of any. Baptism is necessary to salvation, because without it we cannot enter into the kingdom of heaven."[3] One inclined to antiquarian formulations might reply, "Baptism is a sacrament, wherein the washing with water in the Name of the Father, and of the Son, and of the Holy Ghost doth signify and seal our engrafting into Christ, and partakers of the benefits of the covenant of grace, and our engagement to be the Lord's."[4] A less formal but equally traditional respondent might insist that "Baptism is the first and chief sacrament of forgiveness of sins, because it unites us with Christ, who died for our sins and rose for our justification. . . ."[5]

Now, O curious alien, what do you know?

You know as much as most, if not all, the humans gathered at that thing called a "font." Stick around and learn a thing or two about whence the strange rite you and they are witnessing.

Workshop

Luke revisits the persistent first-century notion that the Baptist might have been "the One who was to come." Certainly this reflects a real situation: no doubt a significant number of mid-to-late first-century Jews and Gentiles were assessing the careers of the late John and the late Jesus with an eye to which of the two movements might best reward their loyalty. Luke makes John demur and actually debase himself ("I am not worthy to untie his shoes.") Then, expressing a sentiment that is not typically Lukan, John is made to add all the business about the wheat and the chaff and the unmistakable hint of harsh judgment for those neither astute nor fortunate enough to be adjudged wheat.

Water baptism seems to be played down with John's "I baptize you with water, but. . . ." The real baptism will be "with the Holy Spirit and with fire"—fire being a symbol of judgment and purification. See Malachi 3:2b–3: "For he is like a refiner's fire . . . and he will purify the descendants of Levi and refine them until they present offerings to the Lord in righteousness." Luke will later in "the second book" take the symbol of baptism by fire to new heights in the depiction of baptism/ordination of the apostles at Pentecost, an event that is obliquely referred to in the portion from the Acts of the Apostles (8:14–17) appointed in the Revised Common Lectionary as the second reading before the gospel passage at hand. See also Isaiah 43:2, part of this proper's first appointed reading, and its allusion to both "fire" and "water."

As to the baptism of Jesus, it has long provided a theological puzzlement to those who wish to perpetuate the myth of Jesus' sinlessness—as if he had not been a human being with all the physical and psychic apparatus of *homo sapiens*. John's baptism was (or was depicted as being) for the forgiveness of sin. All four canonical gospels agree that

Jesus was baptized. Of the four, only Mark says so clearly, though he seems to be offering hearsay evidence: "In those days Jesus came from Nazareth of Galilee and was baptized by John in the Jordan."

Matthew has Jesus coming from Nazareth for the purpose of being baptized, but interposes an argument by John about who should baptize whom. Matthew's Jesus prevails, saying in effect that "this will be a good example for others to follow." The Gospel of John suggests (1:31) that the Baptist came baptizing "that he (messiah/Jesus) might be revealed to Israel." John (the evangelist) finesses direct mention of Jesus' baptism at the hands of the Baptist, who is depicted as saying he didn't even know Jesus by sight, but allows him to witness to his own vision of the heavenly epiphany.

Sometimes Jesus' baptism is referred to by theologians as an "embarrassment," since by common consent of four otherwise competing gospel traditions, Jesus was for a time subordinate to John, and, furthermore, considered himself needful of a baptism (washing) meant to remove the mark of sin. That the event is nevertheless included or referred to in one way or another by all four canonical evangelists tells a great many scholars that it must actually have occurred. But why should it not have occurred? John the Baptist seems originally to have been as prominent, if not more so, than Jesus. It may well be that Jesus or a Jesus-type may have been drawn to the charismatic figure of the Baptist and later broke with him ideologically or succeeded him after the Baptist's imprisonment and eventual execution.[6]

John Dominic Crossan has now and again made a point of contrasting the Baptist's evident apocalyptic nature with Jesus' sapiential view—one that envisions the coming of the kingdom (i.e., the reign of justice) not in terms of external portents, but inward qualities. The Baptist is generally depicted as renouncing the world. Jesus is depicted as embracing the world and guiding people in the development of an ethical wisdom to make it a world that could work.

Assuming that a Jesus was among those baptized by John for forgiveness, perhaps it may be said that Jesus (or those writing about him) may have evolved a different meaning of baptism than John or anyone else had intended. Maybe as the image of Jesus matured in the development of the gospels, it came to be seen that forgiveness of sin had less to do with preparation for the end of something than with a new beginning.

Homiletic Commentary

Whatever else the rite of baptism may be, it does draw a line in time between something before and something after. The question in both directions is "What?" The catechisms quoted above in Rubric say that baptism effects a change in and for the baptized from a former state of exclusion to a new one of inclusion—inclusion in a kingdom, covenant, or whatever. A theologian would say it was an "ontological" matter, one concerned with the issue of "being." Before baptism, the person in question "was" something. Now he/she "is" something different.

This is where our E.T. friend would have to shake his head in wonderment. He could easily see that the infant over whom the water of baptism was poured was the same bedewed as unbedewed. If Mr. E.T. were to voice that thought, the priest or minister at the font might tell him that what he saw was "an outward and visible sign of an inward and spiritual grace." E.T. would undoubtedly phone home on the spot, realizing that the infant in question would have no memory of the occasion. The assumption might be that those things promised by the adults involved would, if delivered on, help to produce the ontological or at least the behavioral state envisioned by the rite.

Now imagine that E. T. had dropped into an Episcopal Church that used the 1979 rite and heard these words: QUESTION TO THE SPONSORS OR TO AN ADULT CANDIDATE: "Will you strive for justice and peace among all people, and respect the dignity of every human being?" ANSWER OF SPONSORS OR OF ADULT CANDIDATE: "I will, with God's help."[7]

In that case, E.T. would understand that the strange rite he had witnessed was pointed outward to the world and had to do not with an ontological value but an ethical one. The vow asked and given was to engage the world at the points where justice needed be done and peace needed to be made, beginning with respect for the dignity of every person. Now, E.T. would say to himself, "I see the point of it all. It all rests on those adults who gave the vows for the infant. If they do their job and raise the kid on the values of peace and justice and human dignity, all this was worth it."

Notes

1. "A Catechism," *Book of Common Prayer 1928*, p. 581.

2. "An Outline of the Faith Commonly Called the Catechism," *Book of Common Prayer 1979*, p. 858.

3. "Lesson Fourteen: On Baptism," Questions 152–54, *The Baltimore Catechism*, p. 38.

4. *Westminster Shorter Catechism*, Question 94.

5. "On Baptism for the Forgiveness of Sins,"*Catechism of the Catholic Church* (1992), #977.

6. See Flavius Josephus, *Antiquities of the Jews*, book 18, chap. 5,2.

7. "The Baptismal Covenant," *Book of Common Prayer 1979*, p. 305.

WHO NEEDS SUCH
A RELIGION?

2 Samuel 11:16ff

Nathan said to David . . . "Thus says Yahweh the
God of Israel: I anointed you king over Israel,
and I rescued you from the hand of Saul; I gave you
your master's house, and your master's wives into your
bosom, and gave you the house of Israel and of Judah;
and if that had been too little, I would have added
as much more. Why have you despised the word of
Yahweh, to do what is evil in his sight? You have struck
down Uriah the Hittite with the sword and have taken
his wife to be your wife . . . Now therefore the sword
shall never depart from your house . . ." David said
to Nathan, "I have sinned against Yahweh." Nathan
said to David, "Now Yahweh has put away your sin;
you shall not die. Nevertheless, because by this deed
you have utterly scorned (the enemies of) Yahweh, the
child born to you shall die . . ."

Rubric

It is nothing short of amazing that any people at any time
anywhere would have to do with the deity depicted in this
well-known story and the religion formed around belief
in such a deity. There is not a grace note in the whole tale:
from the unbridled desire of David for Bathsheba, to what
must have been her submission to his power, to David's unsuccessful conniving to cover up the paternity of the child
of his assignation, to Nathan's rehearsal of the outrage and

then his abrupt absolution of David ("Thou shalt not die"), and finally to the offhand comment that, instead of David's life being the divine exacting of revenge it will be that of the innocent child.

Workshop

David must have been in the minds of those who told the story "too big to fail." Yes, he was all too human. Yes, he abused his considerable power as king to steal the wife of his faithful warrior, and then doubled down on that abuse by arranging for his death in the heat of battle, hoping that everyone except, of course, he (David) and Bathsheba would believe that the child to be born was Uriah's. David did not count on Nathan figuring it out.

Bathsheba should not be made out a temptress. She was merely going about the business of either a ritual bath after her menstrual period or a general washing. She is afforded but four words in the entire narrative, leaving the reader to wonder whether she resisted the royal summons or, in another time or culture, might have called what happened rape.

Those four words were, "I am with child," by which message she is depicted as reporting to David via an intermediary the bad news that set in motion David's idiotic and unsuccessful plot to tempt one of his finest and most loyal soldiers to break the taboo of sexual abstinence before battle.

Nathan plays the classic role of the prophet. That is, he discerns what the truth of the matter is and speaks that truth to power—with impunity, as it turns out. Other such prophets—one thinks of Elijah, Amos and Jeremiah—paid dearly for their devotion to doing the prophet's duty. Nathan is made over into a priest toward the end of the story as, in effect, he pronounces an absolution of sorts upon David.

The trouble in the minds of the author(s) is that the sin had to be paid for (as St. Paul would later observe, "The wages of sin is death"—Romans 6:23). Thus, because you can't "off" the king, and even in such a patriarchal society it would be patently unjust to punish Bathsheba beyond what she had already suffered (see Yahweh to Eve at Genesis 3:16), the alternative is to kill off the child. Parenthetically, I have often wondered how the Roman Catholic hierarchy and its opposite numbers in the leadership of evangelical Protestantism would try to rationalize Nathan's off-hand condemnation of the unborn child to save David's skin. Oh, never mind.

The Samuel documents alternate between stories supportive of the Judean monarchy and those that are critical. The text at hand is clearly one of the latter. It reveals a David who is altogether human, who is a schemer and a liar, not to mention a lecher. Shakespeare could hardly have done better, though his Richard III, Henry VIII, and Lear are figures striking for their deep flaws. As sad as David's story is because it involves a child cursed while yet *in utero* and the senseless slaughter of an innocent and faithful soldier of the king, it is yet an important story in that the essential criminality of a figure of great power is deliberately exposed by the storyteller through the character of Nathan.

The name "Nathan," meaning "he (God) has given," is a clue that should not be missed. Not only is Nathan a "nabi" (mouth-piece or speaker of truth) but he is clearly meant to be perceived as one who speaks the truth for Yahweh. What this suggests is that the author(s) of these stories saw truth as the most important characteristic of the deity whom they imagined to exercise control over their past, their present, and their future. Kings would come and go, but as Isaiah would later put it, "The Word of Yahweh will stand forever" (Isaiah 40:8b).

Homiletic Commentary

Institutional religion has thriven on the concepts of sin and righteousness, often claiming for itself the right and responsibility to define both, to absolve the former, and to put on the garment of the latter. When adherents buy into such an analysis, a church or communion or hierarchy is invested with such tremendous psychological power that it can inflict great damage upon the minds and souls of people who take them seriously.

Religious authority has no power except what adherents or worshippers or communicants give it. But that dynamic is not evident to most people. They assume that the power has already been conferred on the rabbi or the priest or the imam, when in fact none of them would have any power at all were if not for the laity ceding it to them.

In traditional catholic Christianity, power is said to flow from the deity to its representative(s) whom various communities ordain or otherwise set apart as the real-time, earthly agents of the invisible deity. But suppose they built a Vatican and nobody came. Suppose a pope said, "Jump," and the people said, "Fat chance." Where would the power be?

At this writing in mid-2010, the Roman Church is facing into a storm over the growing scandal of sexually abusive priests and bishops. That is bad enough, but the worst of it is the irresponsible mismanagement of the situation, the denials and pronouncements that amounted to lies. More and more it appears that the primary authority is no longer the hierarchy but the truth of the matter—truth long suppressed and denied. But, as the figure of the Nathan ("Sent by God") discloses, the truth will out, and those about whom it is told must deal with it.

If there is an ultimate authority, it is truth: truth about ourselves, truth about the world in which we live and move and have our being, truth that leads to truth—that is, to fuller disclosure. No religious authority has the power to contain truth indefinitely, as even Rome has discovered. Likewise, no religious authority has in and of itself the power to effect absolution, with or without acknowledgement of the truth. Truth, not privilege, is the garment of righteousness. Righteousness is the state of being free in the truth (John 8:32).

ANOTHER BATHSHEBA STORY BUT WITH A DIFFERENT ENDING

Luke 7:36–8:3

One of the Pharisees asked Jesus to dine with him. Jesus went; and whilst he was at table, a woman of the city who was a sinner, having heard that he was to dine at the Pharisee's house, brought an alabaster jar of ointment. She stood behind him at his feet, weeping, and she began to wash his feet with her tears and to dry them with her hair . . . the Pharisee was outraged and said to himself, "If this Jesus were really the prophet he pretends to be, he would know what kind of woman is touching him, that she is a sinner." . . . In due course, Jesus said to the Pharisee, "Simon, do you see this woman? . . . Her sins, which were many, have been forgiven; hence, she has demonstrated great love. But the one to whom little is forgiven demonstrates little love." And he said to the woman, "Your sins are forgiven."

Rubric

The subject is sin—that is, unintentionally or deliberately doing wrong, or failing both to discern and do what is right, or aiming at but being unable to hit the mark—and how to handle the problem when it comes to light.

In Luke's story we have three primary actors: the Pharisee who hosts the dinner party, Jesus, an unlikely guest, and "a woman of the city, who was a sinner."

Of what "sin" or "sins" the woman of the city was guilty one can only imagine. Whatever they were, she had evidently found forgiveness for them through some experience with Luke's Jesus not vouchsafed to us, and she pours out her love-filled gratitude upon him right in the middle of a formal dinner. Only Luke the novelist could create such a scene.

A note about the Pharisees: The term "Pharisee" is of uncertain origin, but thought by the main body of scholars to have something to do with the idea of "self separation." The term "perushim" denotes a group of people who stood apart from others in post-Exilic Judaism in their close and meticulous attention to Torah. Torah was what sustained the exiled between the first and second temples. As depicted in Mark, Matthew, and Luke, the Pharisees are compulsively concerned with jots and tittles. In John, they are often called simply "the Jews." In reality, the Pharisees were the precursors of the rabbinical class of post-Second Temple Judaism—Jews sufficiently knowledgeable about the literary tradition of Torah and Talmud to carry their people through the Roman period and the Diaspora. The term "Pharisee" in the synoptic gospels is usually employed in an unfair and disparaging way.

Workshop

In the gospel reading at hand, Luke confected for us a deeply human drama that was clearly meant to illustrate redemption.

The setting is, as has been noted, a Pharisee's dinner table, and already the discerning reader knows what Luke's Jesus will be up against. Luke is hard on the Pharisees as a type and does not appear to appreciate that they were innovators and the real brain trust of first-century CE Judaism (see note above). As such they were attentive to law first and custom afterwards, probably as a defense against criticism that they innovated too much. It was Pharisees, for instance, who helped bring belief in an afterlife to Judaism. Martha is depicted in John 11 as responding to Jesus' note of condolence ("Don't worry, your brother will rise again") by saying, "Yes, yes. I know that he will rise again in the resurrection at the last day." In effect, she was acknowledging the Pharisaic teaching with its roots in Daniel 12:2: "And many of those who sleep in the dust shall awake. . . ."

This story of the Pharisee's dinner party is a set-up for a confrontation. Jesus, who is more iconoclast here than innovator, accepts an invitation to dine at the house of a Pharisee later identified as Simon. Luke none too subtly appears to have joined his own version of a story to one that appears at Mark 14:3–9 with a parallel at Matthew 26:6–13, in both of which Simon is said to be a leper. If Luke knew of the two previous versions, was his changing of the host from leper to Pharisee a wry literary twist? The Gospel of John has its own anointing story at 12:1ff.

The Mark-Matthew version has the woman anointing Jesus' head. Luke's woman and John's Mary of Bethany anoint Jesus' feet. There may be some kind of common source, but in fine and typical style Luke elevates the incident to a sublime plane in which love, forgiveness, and peace are primary values. Luke has Jesus point out in 7:44b–46 the social slights Simon visited upon him, suggesting that the hospitality of the table was false and shallow. Eating together in the Mediterranean culture is to this day a sign of high fellowship.

So from the beginning the scene is surreal. It is made the more so by the surprise entrance of "a woman in the city, who was a sinner." A few commentators suggest she was a deliberate plant by Simon to tempt and/or to discredit Jesus, but nothing in the text seems to support that speculation.

The presence of the Greek "kataklithā" in the text (meaning "to recline") tells us that the meal was a formal banquet as reclining at the table was a custom reserved for such an occasion. That would have had Jesus and the other guests lying, side of head on elbow, feet extended away from the food. The woman is depicted as coming up from behind him and letting her tears (of sadness? of penitence? of relief? of joy?) fall upon his feet. She lets her hair down—a most forward act—and uses her tresses to dry his feet. A more sensual scene is not to be found elsewhere in the New Testament. She then anoints his feet: a mark of honor for one who is considered important.

Simon thinks that Jesus ought to know from her brash forwardness what sort of woman is touching him. Simon must have given his thoughts away by the look on his face, because Jesus confronts him, telling him an on-the-spot parable about a creditor and two debtors. The parable is preceded by Jesus' announcement: "Simon, I've got something to say to you." In our own contemporary idiom it would sound as if Jesus is exasperated. Simon, undaunted, responds, "Teacher (*didaskale*): speak your mind." Like *epistata* (master), *didaskale* should be a term of great respect. I think we are entitled to hear it as if Simon spoke it with a sneer, as in, "OK, wise guy, what's on your mind?"

The parable's twist is that one to whom much is forgiven will love the agent of forgiveness more than the one to whom little is forgiven. That would depend, of course, on a debtor's perception of his debt. Certainly, a great debt suddenly forgiven can produce in the debtor a great show of relief and gratitude. So we may infer that the unnamed woman had been carrying around a great burden. She was, after all, "a woman in the city, who was a sinner," obviously known widely as such. Luke appears to want us to think that in some way the woman had already been shriven by some prior contact with Jesus, or that he could not fail to be moved to forgiveness by such extravagant penance. Forgiveness is a large issue for Luke (see 15:11–32).

In Luke's imagination, Simon's other guests were wondering how such a "sinner" could be let off the hook so easily. When Luke depicts Jesus saying to the woman "Your sins are forgiven" the Greek used is the term *apheōnātai*, meaning approximately that her sins had already been forgiven and therefore in the present remain forgiven. Luke wants to leave the impression that Simon's friends perceive Jesus himself to have pronounced absolution.

The first three verses of chapter 8, which are thematically unrelated to 7:36–50, constitute what I take to be a deliberate attempt by the lectionary's editors to connect Mary Magdalene to the dinner story. She is named in 8:2 as one of three named women who joined the twelve in following Jesus through the next set of towns and villages. Still, it is highly doubtful that the author of Luke meant to suggest Mary Magdalene as the unnamed "woman of the city."

Homiletic Commentary

The woman in question in our present text, who may well have been a victim of male abuse of power, was forgiven—as if she had any choice in the matter of her violation. Perhaps without that public show of forgiveness, she would have met the end that many Middle Eastern women meet even to this day for having been raped: public humiliation, beating, and possibly death.

If that was her story, she had not "sinned much" but had been much sinned against. In any event, her forgiveness (that is to say, restoration to the human race) was as great in the positive as her degradation would have been in the negative.

Whatever forgiveness is, it is certainly not the act of an invisible deity. It is, rather, the embrace of wrongdoers or of the wrong-done-to. It is the reaching out to the offender and the offended alike in an effort to sew the tattered garment of the human community back together into some

semblance of wholeness without which life is mere exis-
tence in diminishment.

For a very long time, Roman Catholics were forbidden
receipt of communion if they had not had their slate of sins
cleared by a priestly absolution. The ecclesiology was that
the holy table was a place for the holy, and the unshriven
sinner was unholy. In theory, that is good ecclesiology. In
practice, it is defective. Sometimes it is the fellowship of the
table, however gained, that discloses the state of forgiveness—or so it is suggested by the tale of the "woman in the
city, who was a sinner" coming uninvited to dinner at the
Pharisee's house.

NOT LOOKING BACK ON THE ROAD LESS TRAVELED BY

Luke 9:51–62

When the time came for Jesus to be taken up, he set his jaw to go to Jerusalem. He sent messengers on ahead of him. They went first to a Samaritan village where the people would have nothing to do with them because they were headed toward Jerusalem. A couple of Jesus' followers wondered aloud if they should call heaven's fire down upon those people. Jesus silenced them. As they continued down the road, someone came up to Jesus and said, "I want to follow you wherever you're going." Jesus told him that if he did so, he would be essentially homeless. To another person, Jesus merely said, "Follow me." This person said, "First let me go attend to the burial of my father," to which Jesus replied, "Let the dead bury their own. Let us go and proclaim the rule of God." Yet another person said he wanted to join up but he had to go home and say goodbye to his family first. Jesus said to him, "No one who puts his hand to the plow and then looks back is fit for this work."

Rubric

The theme is following; the verb, "to follow." The idea is that an invitation of great consequence may come only once, at least with that first sunburst of new opportunity. Then it is not enough to say, "Not now. Later. I have other things to do." Or as Luke quotes Jesus saying to the interested but still reluctant, "No one who puts a hand to the plow and then looks back is fit for the realm of God"—that is, for the rule that puts others above self, demands unconditional love of enemy as well as neighbor, requires permanent willingness to walk a second mile and take off the shirt as well as the coat and give it away, and enjoins all sorts of countercultural behavior that may mark one as an unredeemable eccentric otherwise known as a disciple of Jesus.

The ones who wanted to bury their dead got the point. They knew they might not come back. Thus also for those who wanted to bid farewell to family. That hesitation was the natural human desire to cling to important relationships and what must be done to maintain them in loving and accountable ways.

That is the crossroads at which would-be disciples ever stand: between the past and present that are known and comfortable, and the future that is unsure and therefore threatening. One either goes or does not go. Robert Frost said he took the road less traveled by,[1] and that made all the difference. Luke says Jesus "set his face to go to Jerusalem," and any way one looks at the story that unfolds from there, a great difference was made.

Workshop

Chapter 9, verse 51 is the point of departure for Luke's Jesus as he begins what over most of the next 10 chapters (to 18:36) will be his second journey to Jerusalem, the first being a family trip narrated in Luke 2:22–51. Mark and Matthew more or less agree on the single Jerusalem trip of the adult Jesus. The Gospel of John deals with elapsed time in a different framework, in which Jesus makes not one but three trips to Jerusalem.

Luke's itinerary for Jesus will sometimes seem to illustrate Zeno's paradox because here and there it seems to stall and almost terminate. But here at 9:51, Luke makes certain that readers know how fateful the journey will turn out to be and how clearly Jesus seemed to know it. In verse 51 Luke (literally) says of Jesus that he "set his face stiffly" toward Jerusalem. Think here of a set jaw, a look of utter determination mixed with anxiety over what may await him there. The author of Luke was certainly not a witness to whatever Jesus' last days may have held, but here he captures what surely must have been their emotional content.

Chapter 9, verses 51–56 are unique, with no clear parallels in Mark or Matthew. For Luke, the way from Galilee would go through Samaria, to which Jesus sent messengers (*aggeloi*) perhaps to set up camp for the night or to arrange lodging.

The running feud between North and South, with which Luke subsequently deals in 10:30–37 (The Good Samaritan), intervenes to keep Jesus on the move (see 9:53). James and John evidently believed they had power similar to that which Elijah is depicted as using to embarrass the prophets of Baal (see 1st Kings 18). The two asked Jesus if they might torch the Samaritans' houses and them as well. Perhaps Luke has Jesus reject such a course of action in order to distinguish him from John the Baptist and Elijah, both of whom were fiery reformers.

Matthew and Luke share the next scene, in which a person approaches Jesus in the course of the journey to volunteer discipleship (v. 57). For Matthew, it is a scribe; for Luke simply "someone" who says, "I will follow you wherever you go." In echoes of Luke 9:21–26, Luke's Jesus says to the person that membership in the project he seeks to join comes with the assurance of such serious deprivation as having no permanent bed of one's own. To yet another would-be disciple (in Matthew that other person is already a disciple), Jesus lays down the challenge: "Follow me." And as if to prove that discipleship will always cost more than most can bear, Luke has the prospective disciple ask to defer his commitment until a dead father can be buried.

In both Luke and Matthew, Jesus is made to say, "Let the dead bury their own dead." Much has been written about this proverb-like saying. In Luke's time it may have meant something like, "Those who have not answered the call are as good as dead. May as well bury them."

To the one who wants to follow, but only after he goes home to say farewell, Jesus is made to say: "No one who first puts his hand to the plow and then looks back is fit material for the rule of God." In other words, the one doing the plowing must keep his eye fixed on the ground before him in order to plow a straight and usable furrow. Pushing a plow forward whilst looking backward would be a sign of ineptness and stupidity.

With that gauntlet thrown down, Jesus, with a look of fixed determination in his jaw, is off to Jerusalem and to whatever it has to offer. He has set his hand to the plow, and he will not look back, much less go back.

Homiletic Commentary

The trouble with most of contemporary Christianity is that its path takes one down the road most frequently traveled. It is rutty and predictable from long and repeated use. It leads to nowhere in particular at little to no cost. One can take it or leave it, and there is not much difference either way. For that reason alone, there is not much hope that a study session or homily on this text will be more than an academic exercise, and probably a fairly low-wattage one at that.

That is because the prophetic lineaments of the Jewish-Christian stream of thought are treated mostly as a matter of history rather than a call to action in the present.

Beneath the pious veneer of the gospels lies the story of a first-century subversive movement not unlike what Mohandas Gandhi's would turn out to be in the first half of the twentieth century: one of passive resistance that drove the authorities crazy. The movement that grew up around the countercultural ethical wisdom attributed to a "Jesus of Nazareth" was neither a military one nor in ordinary terms a political one. It was made up of people who were trying to live with each other and the world according to the terms of Hillel's and Jesus' Golden Rule of not treating others as one would not want to be treated, of people who were bound and determined to love their enemies into friends, of people geared up to turn the other cheek to the smiter. Yet the effect was a political one, and Rome tried to quash it and, after a fashion, succeeded.

One objects, saying, "The Christian church is alive and well today. So Rome did not succeed." Really? "Rome" will have succeeded beyond its wildest dreams unless and until those who would be disciples of Jesus as he is depicted in the gospels set their faces en masse toward the seat of power, there to insist by example on peace instead of war and on distributive rather than retributive justice.

As a veteran of the civil rights and anti-war movements of the last half century, I can tell you that passive insistence, like passive resistance, is carried out at a price. Those who are already essentially dead from their repetitive journeys down the well-known, spirit-numbing road oft taken need fear no more than a nominal charge for their trip—save burial in the minutiae of routine. The road less traveled by takes one to his own Jerusalem where awaits the establishment that is sure to strike back at passive insistence.

There's one other reason why having first put his hand to the plow one should not look back. Often enough, he will find himself alone.

Notes

1. "The Road Not Taken," *Complete Poems of Robert Frost* (Henry Holt and Co., 1949), p. 131.

NEIGHBORS AND
NEIGHBORHOODS

Luke 10:25–37

A lawyer tested Jesus by asking him, "What do I have to do to guarantee eternal life for myself?" Jesus put the question back on him, saying, "What is written in the law? What do you read there?" The lawyer quoted Leviticus 19:18, the commandment requiring love of neighbor as self. Jesus praised his answer and advised the lawyer to do just that. But the lawyer wanted a definition of "neighbor." Jesus replied, "A man was going down from Jerusalem to Jericho where he encountered a gang of robbers who took his clothes, beat him badly and left him to die. Now as it happened a priest was going down that road and saw the man, and walked around him to the other side of the road. Likewise a Levite. But a Samaritan traveling on the same road came upon the man and took pity on him, bandaged and dressed his wounds, and took him to a hostel. He told the host to take care of him and handed over two days' wages to pay for it and promised to cover any further expenses that might be incurred until he returned." Jesus asked the lawyer which of the three had been a neighbor to the victim?" The lawyer said, "The one who had mercy on him." Jesus told him to "go and do likewise."

Rubric

Among the best known passages of religious literature are the verses of Luke that constitute what is known as "the parable of the Good Samaritan." It is so regarded because its compelling plot is one to which people of all sorts and conditions can and do relate. Like the classic parable, it means one thing at one time and one thing at another. It means one thing now, but it will mean something different next time around. One thing it doesn't mean is that the priest and his acolyte, the Levite, were bad people. They were just trying to get to where they had to go in order to do what they were obligated to do, and to do so uncontaminated by blood and death in accordance with the commandments (see Numbers 5:2ff, Leviticus 15).

The parable hangs there in spatial and temporal suspension, just as a dissonant chord awaits resolution that does not come. The hearer is invited to resolve it if and as he can—or not.

Workshop

Talk about midrash. Talk about the living word. With this passage of eight concise verses, we encounter Luke at his gospel's finest moment as it shows how near the "rule of God" can be when and where it is least expected. The so-called Parable of the Good Samaritan is Luke's imaginative extension of a colloquy between Jesus and a lawyer, an exchange reported in some form by all three synoptic gospels.

In Matthew's version, Jesus' questioner is a Pharisee, in Mark a scribe. At issue in the Matthean exchange is which of the 613 commandments of Torah is the greatest; in Mark which commandment is the first (in importance); and in Luke what must be accomplished to inherit eternal life—a term meaning not life without end but life in its fullest possibilities here and now, a matter of quality rather than mere length. The answer in each case is the commandment to love God first and foremost (Deuteronomy 6:5) followed by the admonition to love neighbor as self (Leviticus 19:18).

Luke handles the inquiry differently than do Mark and Matthew by having Jesus turn the question back upon the

lawyer: v. 26, "What is written in the law? How do you read
it?" It may remind one of a Supreme Court justice question-
ing a lawyer before the bar. But the lawyer is not about to
allow his questioner (in this case Luke's Jesus) to make a
point at his expense, and so poses another question in an attempt to justify his initial inquiry—which was not a stupid
question, given the sometimes bitter divisions between and
among different strains of folk in the Levant. The lawyer
was not a dumbbell. He knew the answer to Jesus' post-
parable counter question: "Which of these three, do you
think, was the neighbor to him who fell among thieves?"

The lawyer, presumably associated in some way with the
scribes and Pharisees, could probably not bring himself to
speak the word "Samaritan." And that is one unmistakable
point of the parable. "Samaritan = neighbor? Impossible."

Under "the rule of God," that is to say a world in which
the Hillel Doctrine of not doing to another what one hates,
neighbors are not subject to distinctions or discrimination
among class, clan, kith, and kin. Neighbors are made at the
intersection of need and resource. The late George Arthur
Buttrick wrote of this parable, "People may live divided
only by a narrow wall, and yet not be neighbors. People
may live with no intervening wall, and yet not be neighbors."[1]

When need is served by available resource unstintingly
provided, the result is what the gospels call "the rule of
God." It is as if the commandments mellowed into the
humanist ethic credited by the same gospels to Jesus of
Nazareth. When the lawyer asked what he needed to do to
inherit eternal life (as if it were already his by will and testament), he was asking what was necessary to realize "the
rule of God." The answer was a call to break down such
barriers as exist between, say, Samaritans and Judeans.

What was true of that barrier during the first century CE
was that Judeans thought of themselves as pure Jews as

opposed to the Samaritans to the north whose ancestors had intermarried with Assyrians in earlier centuries. To the Judean, therefore, the Samaritan was tref—unclean. But the Samaritan of the parable was unconcerned with such barriers and fell to the task at hand with the man who was left half dead.

As has been observed above, the story is not a polemic against priests and their assistants over matters of ritual propriety. To avoid rendering himself unfit for priestly activity, a priest could bury only members of his immediate family. The Levite, a member of a kind of "associate priest" class, would have been under similar restrictions. Is Luke saying that such restrictions are invalidated by emergent need? Or is it a more general head shaking, inviting the inference that no job is so vital that a person on the way to doing it should fail to lend a hand?

The parable reveals nothing about the Samaritan's identity other than that he was of and from Samaria—and by inference has all the perceived faults attendant upon his origin.

Either way, the Samaritan might have had nothing to lose in any formal, cultic sense by coming to the unfortunate robbery victim's aid. Though thinking of that road from Jerusalem down to Jericho with its drop of almost 1800 feet over a mere dozen miles through crag and rocky paths, why wouldn't the robbers of Luke's imagination be lurking for another victim upon whom to pounce? So personal risk was a real issue for him as well.

What in Luke's imagination would have been the motivation for the Samaritan to turn aside to administer first aid? And then to convey the victim to a hostel and leave the equivalent of two days' wages for his care with a promise to return with more if needed?

By indirection, Luke answered his own question thus: Those who have little to lose, or who wear what they have lightly enough that to risk losing some or even all of it, are the kind of people who can turn a crime scene into a neighborhood. "Go and do likewise," is what Jesus is made to say to the lawyer, who surely must have been sorry he ever asked his question in the first place.

Homiletic Commentary

If it is accurate to say that this parable hangs, as suggested above, in spatial and temporal suspension like a dissonant chord awaiting resolution, how shall it be resolved? Or can it be?

In 2010 the possibilities for resolution are as numerous and they are nearly impossible to imagine. How does the abyss separating the aspirations of the Israeli from those of the Palestinian get bridged? How can the conflicting views of the Arab or Pakistani jihadi be harmonized with those of the typical middle-class American Christian? How can the political analysis of the socialist-leaning Democrat be reconciled with those of staunch political and economic conservatives?

The barrier between Samaritan and Judean (if that is the division Luke was thinking of) was crossed and removed in a simple act of kindness and mercy by what must have been risky in more ways than one. For a Judean to be so tenderly cared for by a Samaritan would have involved the shame of being touched by defiled hands. For the Samaritan thus to stop and occupy himself was to expose himself to the same fate as the one suffered by the person he was trying to save. To part with two days' worth of wages was then and would be today no small investment in the life of a stranger who under ordinary circumstances would consider the agent of mercy a dirty dog.

Here, then, I will go out on the proverbial limb; here in the late Spring of 2010 let me tell you how I choose to resolve the dissonance. At this writing I will say that in Luke's imagination, the Good Samaritan must have been the avatar of all the human potential for good and loveliness Luke believed was realizable. And if it could be manifest on a lonely and perilous mountain pass infested with robbers who cared not how and where they obtained their loot, it could be manifest anywhere. And that in turn means that emergent need must always trump ideology as well as racial, cultural, social, and economic identity.

Edna St. Vincent Millay may have said it most memorably: "Heaven was a neighbor's house, Open flung to us, bereft."[2]

Notes

1. *The Parables of Jesus* (Harper & Brothers, 1928), p. 152.
2. "The Blue-Flag in the Bog," *Second April*, by Edna St. Vincent Millay (Harper & Brothers, 1935), p.3.

EATING AND HEALING:
THE NEW TESTAMENT'S
RELIGION

1 Kings 17:1–24

Elijah had been lying low near a running brook named Cherith, comfortable in the cool grass and provided with his meals morning and evening by a flock of ravens. He also drank from the clear waters of the brook. One day the brook dried up due to lack of rain. Yahweh then sent Elijah to Zarephath to visit a widow there who was to provide his food. When he got there he asked the widow for water and also for a morsel of bread. The widow responded by saying she had nothing but a handful of meal in a jar and a small amount of oil in the cruse—just enough to make a loaf of bread for herself and her son—probably their last meal, as a famine was upon them. Still, the widow complied and made a loaf for Elijah, but that did not deplete the meal in the barrel or the oil in the cruse. Thereupon the son of the widow fell ill and had stopped breathing. The widow upbraided Elijah, but he took her son into an upper room where be stretched himself out on top of the child three times, all the while beseeching Yahweh to send life back in to the lad's body. And so it came to pass. The widow said to Elijah: "Now I know that you are a man of God, and that the word of Yahweh is upon your lips."

Luke 7:11–17

Jesus went to a town called Nain, and his disciples along with a large crowd of people went with him. As he neared the gate of the town, he was approached by a cortege bearing the body of a man who had died. He had been the only son of his mother. When the Lord saw her, he was filled with great empathy and said, "Please don't cry." He approached and touched the bier and said, "Young man, I say to you, rise." The dead man sat up and began to speak. The crowd was spooked, but claimed that "a great prophet" had come among them. That word was spread throughout the province of Judea and beyond.

Rubric

Eating together and healing—both verb forms in this case—are characteristic of the activities of early apostolic Christianity. They are featured in Luke 10:1–12, the mission of the 70 who are to "go to every town" where they are to take room and board with those whose maladies they are to heal. The two activities are joined in the narrative about Elijah and the widow of Zarephath, which is, in turn, linked thematically to Luke 7:11–17 wherein yet another healing narrative involves a widow's son.

Workshop

Luke sets the story in a lower Galilean village called "Nain," which may be the contemporary "Nein," about five miles southeast of Nazareth and 25 from Capernaum. Nain (or Nein) rates no other mention in canonical Hebrew or Christian scripture.

A number of sites—junctions of old roads in what were the Confederate States of America—are remembered solely for decisive battles fought at them. Otherwise no one would have bothered to name them. What is said to have occurred at Nain/Nein gives the place its textual fame. It was at the gate of that place that Luke depicts Jesus encountering a funeral procession. The deceased is said to be a widowed mother's only son. No one asks anything of Jesus, but according to Luke he was moved with compassion (*esplagchnisthā*—a gut-level wrenching of emotion) and pleads with the woman not to cry. He says, "Young man, I say to you, 'Be roused from sleep.'" It is a faint echo of the elohim speaking light into being.

The scene presages the later narrative in John's gospel of the raising of Lazarus, in which case John clearly means the reader to understand that Lazarus was dead—hence the reference to the olfactory evidence. In any event, the widow's son, supposed to be dead, "sat up and began to speak."

The fact that speech is depicted as the first true sign of re-animation says plenty. It connects speaking with what will come to be known as "resurrection." Even though he does not give the re-animated man actual words to speak, you can bet that Luke meant for those he made witnesses of the event to speak of it far and wide—just as gospel communities, post-70 CE, spread the word of Jesus' "resurrection" (however the "truth" of that report was understood). It was what distinguished their brand of Judaism from most synagogue or continuing post-Temple Judaism.

And to be sure, Luke 7:17 assures us that word of the event did spread throughout Judea and environs, just as the "resurrection" story afterwards did by other means during the church's formative years. And the very next verse says, "The disciples of John (the Baptist) reported all these things to him," a report that caused John to send a deputation to Jesus to ask if he was "The One." The reply was, in effect, "Judge me by what you see has happened."

The Revised Common Lectionary provides with this gospel the reading from 1 Kings 17 in which Elijah is depicted as bringing a widow's son back to life, albeit by more than just a spoken word. The obvious connection between Zarephath and Nain is the proclamation of the funeral cortege to the effect that "a great prophet has risen among us" and the widow of Zarephath's exclamation that he who mooched the last handful of her flour and drops of her oil (both of which were miraculously replenished "for many days") was now to be seen as "a man of God, and that the word of Yahweh in your mouth is truth." That latter is the spot-on description of a prophet, great or otherwise.

Homiletic Commentary

The story is that Elijah claimed to have been directed by Yahweh to take up residence beside a brook named "Cherith," there to be saved from the depredations of a drought and consequent famine. And there Elijah will not only dwell beside a pleasant flow of potable water to slake his thirst and cool his brow; his board will also be provided by a flock of ravens who will bring him bread and meat each morning and evening.

Some patient research of this text suggests that the Hebrew word "Cherith" means something like "separate," and the ravens may have been members of servile tribe afraid or a little in awe of Elijah, a fabled public intellectual in antiquity. Take the text in light of twenty-first-century realities, and you have a pampered elite living in a gated community, being waited on hand and foot (or talon and beak, if you wish not to rationalize the ravens). Elijah is separated from the sufferings of the world beyond the lush confines of his brook until . . . until it comes to pass one day that the brook dries up and — though the text does not specify it — the ravens come no more.

That very kind of thing happened in America not so long ago as fabulous fortunes gained on the backs of so-called ordinary citizens were vaporized in a cloud of greedy over-reach. For a while, the haves lost access to their brook, and their ravens took to flight.

But back to Elijah, who is now brook-less and raven-less, and no doubt hungry, frazzled, and not a little annoyed. The text says he heard Yahweh's voice directing him to a village later known as Serapta on the Phoenician coast of the Mediterranean. If the brook Cherith is where we think it was—near Gilead—it would have been quite a hike to undertake with parched tongue and on an empty stomach—roughly 80 miles as the raven flies and discounting any hills.

Elijah must have wondered what he had done to deserve that. In any event, the text asks us to believe he went there, only to discover a widow gathering kindling for a fire over which to cook her and her son's last meal, so devastated were they by the famine. Now comes this stranger to want, asking to be cut in.

You can imagine the conversation: "Who are you?" / "I am the man who has been residing in a far country by a cool running brook and the ravens brought me breakfast and dinner." / "Really? Did you ever ask anybody to join you?" / "No, I didn't. I was kind of in hiding, unsure of what would come next. But yesterday, the brook dried up and the ravens went away." / "Oh, did they really?" she says, not really meaning it as a question. / "Yes, and now I am hungry," Elijah says. / "YOU'RE hungry? Here I am," the widow says, "scraping the bottom of my flour bin to make one last loaf for my son and me before we die of hunger. And you, who lay by the Brook Cherith with the ravens feeding you—YOU'RE hungry??????"

Evidently impervious to embarrassment, Elijah pulled himself up to the widow's table for what turned out to be nobody's last meal. Surely Elijah had not come away from Cherith without some remnant of the ravens' twice-daily offerings tucked into his rucksack against the coming and going of a mealtime. We are permitted to assume that he added from his relative plenty to the widow's well-nigh absolute want, and, behold, a partnership in sufficiency was forged that saved their three lives.

Elijah was not a Lady Bountiful but presented himself as a member of the family, sharing at table what little he had with the widow, who shared what little she had. Then he stuck around long enough to do what was necessary to preserve the life that meal had sustained. Therein is the template of righteousness.

THE NECESSARY THING

Luke 10:38–42

As Jesus and his disciples continued on their way, they came to a village where they were welcomed into the home of two sisters, Martha and Mary. While Martha was in the kitchen preparing a meal for her guest, her sister Mary sat with Jesus, hanging on his every word. Driven to distraction by all she had to do, Martha interrupted Jesus to ask whether he was unaware of her labors and her sister's having deserted her, and to suggest that he might do well to order Mary into the kitchen. Jesus patiently chided her, "Martha, Martha: take it easy. Don't worry so much about the details. Focus on the better part your sister has chosen. I will not have it taken from her."

Rubric

This reading from Luke with its story of Jesus' drop-in visit to the residence of Mary and Martha raises three primary issues: a) what it meant at the beginnings of Jesus Judaism or nascent Christianity to be a follower, b) the imperative that the passage of finite time lays upon those purposefully on the way toward crisis and c) the importance of the servant role.

The story belongs alone to the Lukan document, lacking any parallel in other gospels, as is also true for the parable of the Good Samaritan, which immediately precedes it. No first-century CE writer was better at storytelling than whoever Luke was. His stories always display color and movement; they are not icons or vignettes, but have almost the character of short film clips. One can hear the exasperation in Martha's voice and the firm patience in Jesus'. One can see Mary looking up into the face of her teacher, unaware and maybe even uncaring of the bustle about her. These details make the story memorable.

If the church could ever re-think its pedagogy and turn homily-time into a seminar-like discussion, a homilist could "teach" this story much in the same manner as a professor of literature teaches an act or a scene from "Hamlet" or one of Shakespeare's sonnets.

However, church still pretty much means people sitting in auditorium-like rows, faces lifted to a pulpit and its preacher in one-way, take-it-or-leave-it communication. What follows in Workshop and Homiletic Commentary can be used as fodder for both homily preparation and group study.

Workshop

More mistaken and unhelpful sermons—and I suppose Sunday school lessons—have been committed using this passage than, wishing to fend off depression, we dare attempt to count. It has been my misfortune to hear many a homily or lesson that used the text to offer women one of two roles: 1) the busy domestic or 2) the silent, adoring type who sits at the feet or her male master.

One can only guess what Luke was up to in crafting this story beyond reminding the reader that a journey is in progress (the leitmotif of Luke). See v. 38—"another village." But the one broad hint that should not go untaken is the clear depiction of Mary as a disciple. (Attention: Vatican! Attention: Anglican and other non-Roman objectors to women's ordination.) Part of being a "disciple"—derived from the Greek μαθητής that came into English via

Latin as *discipulus* means one who learns with or from a teacher.

Thus part of being a disciple (male or female) is listening to what the teacher has to say, and that is what Mary is clearly depicted as doing in the scene Luke created. In the passage previous to this one the lawyer wanted to know what he had to do to inherit eternal life—and having further pressed the point by asking who his neighbor was, he got an answer: "Don't treat your perceived enemy as an enemy but as a neighbor." That's one way to be a disciple of Jesus. Another is to arrange one's life as Mary arranged hers: to be available to the teacher when he was available to her and not to be distracted by other matters, however pressing.

The teacher in this case being a male and the disciple female does not efface what may be the main point of the story—namely, that at least one disciple was depicted as being a woman, the gender pool from which traditionalists insist Jesus did not choose his original inner circle of followers.

In verse 41 Luke's Jesus says that Mary had chosen "the better part," though the adjective at that place means "good" and can be taken as either comparative or superlative. Most English translations have it "the better part" because on the face of it there seemed to have been only two choices: serving or listening. There were, of course, other choices, and some would be "good." Would others have been "bad" or simply "not so good?"

Luke's Jesus called Mary's disposition to listen to him "the good or better part," meaning at the very least that Martha's choice was the "not so good part." In fact, Luke has Jesus tell Martha that "one thing is necessary." Luke's Jesus was not saying that cooking and serving weren't or couldn't be part of discipleship. It depends on how and for whom one undertakes such tasks, and to what end. In any community, a division of labor is vital to its well being. Somebody needs to be in the supply tent preparing dinner just as others need to be listening to the leader. Timing is everything.

Another way of understanding the gentle scolding of Martha is to be found later in Luke at 22:27, at which point Luke gives Jesus this line to speak: "I am among you as one who serves." That is the payoff line in his remonstration with the disciples over who is the greatest among them. Perhaps Luke's Jesus is making the same point by telling Martha, in effect, "I'll get something to eat myself. I don't want to be fawned over. Just come over here and listen to what I'm saying." Read that way, the verse suggests a degree of urgency about it all, suggests that Jesus might not have much time. Luke knew the end of the story Mark had crafted at an earlier time, and according to that account Jesus did not in fact have much time.

Therefore, despite the amenities required by the hospitality code of first-century Palestine, we understand that Jesus did not come to the sisters' home to stay. He had already set his jaw determinedly toward Jerusalem, where Luke's drama will culminate. The purpose of stopping in to see Martha and Mary was not to sample the cuisine. If the depiction of Mary means what it says, the stop had more to do with the making of a disciple. Martha was not incorrect in her actions. She was as correct as Simon the Pharisee (see Luke 7:36–50) had been incorrect. In Luke's plot, it was just that Martha didn't understand what Jesus was doing in her house.

Homiletic Commentary

The life of many Christian communities, especially those in settled and relatively prosperous locales, generally tends to be dilatory and ho-hum—as if not too much is at stake or at risk, as if Point A. had not been departed from and Point B. were not looming ever closer.

Certainly the church has business, and much of it is usual as well as necessary. But that business is to be done in support of the mission. The business is not the mission. The church, like Luke's Martha, has become adept and efficient at its business but utterly neglectful of its mission. The church has no time for a seven-course feast. It needs to grab a granola bar and get on with it, but not before listening to the voice of its leader and hero who knew the way (a hard one), the truth (a piercing one), and the life (a sacrificial one).

PRAYER IS AS PRAYER DOES

Luke 11:1–13

J esus was praying as was his wont, and after he was finished, one of his disciples asked him to teach him and his fellow disciples to pray, as John (the Baptizer) had taught his. So Jesus said, "Pray like this: say, 'Father, your name is holy. May your rule take hold. Give us the food we need for today. Forgive what we do wrong as we forgive those who have done us wrong. Do not put us on trial.'" He said further, "Suppose you go to your friend late at night and ask him to lend you three loaves of bread because company arrived late at your house. You know he's going to tell you to go away because the door is locked and everybody is in bed. But you know that if you stand there long enough, he will get out of bed and give you what you asked for. So when it comes to praying, try this: Ask, and you will be given it. Search, and you will find it. Knock on the door, and it will be opened to you. If your child asked for a fish, would you give him a snake? Or if for an egg, would you give him a scorpion? Well, then, why would your Father in heaven not give you the Holy Spirit to anyone who asks?"

Rubric

Prayer, as an activity, is generally associated with piety and the pious. Its practice is thought to be a virtue connected with humility. In most religions, the pray-er is expected to present himself in a certain posture, e.g. kneeling or prostrate or hands and arms lifted in petition. Yet, the narrative of Genesis 18:22–33 depicts a negotiation between Abraham and Yahweh over the fate of Sodom and Gomorrah. Likewise in the so-called institution of "the Lord's prayer," the activity of petition seems far less an expression of piety than of moral and practical demand, though generally veiled in salaamic deference.

In some ways, the Sodom-Gomorrah negotiation is one of the most humorous passages in the Bible. Yahweh's patience level is tested again and again as Abraham whittles down the required number of righteous ones in the threatened cities to a minyan (a "count" in Hebrew, but usually meaning ten). Abraham asks for what he wants and gets it. Mercy was Yahweh's to give; it was Abraham's to receive. An interesting equation, in which x plus y equals justice— or at the very least, mercy.

Workshop

By all accounts, the type of prayer Jesus regularly practiced seems to have been of the meditative sort—a kind of inner musing, seeking solace and guidance with a clearer head, with seldom so much as a "let this cup pass from me" type of petition. Taking that into consideration suggests that Luke's Jesus taught his disciples to pray in yet another way: in a series of imperatives.

As conceived of by Jews from the earliest times, the God of Abraham, Isaac, and Jacob demanded human attention, which, because one could not "see" Yahweh on the pain of death, had to be given remotely through the medium of prayer—that is, by human beings addressing the unseen yet perceived deity. Long before Luke (or Mark or Matthew) sat down to write their narratives, Judaism had a well-established tradition of formal prayers. Presumably the disciples knew of that tradition.

What apparently they had witnessed, as Luke tells the story, was Jesus absorbed from time to time in meditative solitude. Can we presume that was John the Baptizer's practice, as well? Did the unnamed disciple who asked Jesus to teach him and his fellows to pray know how and what the Baptizer's following had been taught? And were the prayer patterns used by John and Jesus both departures from the norm of established, formal prayers?

In the disciple's request, literally "Lord, teach us to pray as John taught his disciples," the use of "Lord" strongly suggests a post-crucifixion setting, because in New Testament writings "Lord" is the name or title for Jesus used by later first-century CE Jesus Jews, an appellative by which they meant "the resurrected one."

In any event, according to Luke's Jesus, the addressee of the prayer is to be "abba," a familiar and somewhat intimate form of address to one's male parent. The prescribed form of the prayer, since the spokes-disciple asked, was to be as follows: an affirmation of the promise that the hallowed deity's rule will dawn, requests for daily bread and absolution of the stain of wrongdoing dependent in some way upon granting the same absolution to those who have affronted the pray-er. Matthew's use of "debts" instead of "sins" or "trespasses" is closer to a first-century CE Palestinian understanding of remission. And Matthew places the requisite action on our part in the past tense: "As we have forgiven our debtors."

It is interesting to observe that the Markan parallel (11:25–26) to Luke 11:1–4 and Matthew 6:9–13) refers only to forgiveness: "And whenever you stand praying, forgive if you have a thing against another." For Mark that forgiveness is requisite "so that your Father . . . may forgive you."

The final petition is that the pray-er may not be put to the test—that is, should not be faced with the necessity of choosing faithfulness and dying for it. Don't forget the perilous conditions under which most Jesus Jews lived during the last third of the first century CE.

Perhaps to illustrate the efficacy of prayer, Luke turns a parable of persistence (11:5–8) into an object lesson that is unique to his gospel. The story is that a traveler journeying by night, perhaps to avoid the heat of the day, arrives at a friend's house and begs entry. The householder has no bread to put before the weary traveler in accordance with the code of Mediterranean hospitality. So the unprepared host goes next door and importunes a friend who has long since retired and is asleep with his family gathered to him. The would-be host to the traveler asks for bread. The neighbor does not wish to be disturbed, but after enduring persistent requests, he gives in.

The pattern for that kind of persistence derives from the legend of Abraham's bargaining with Yahweh for Sodom and Gomorrah. One is not approaching a tyrant but a father or brother figure. One comes to press for the fulfillment of a desire. It may have been St. Thomas Aquinas who said that it is legitimate to pray for that which it is legitimate to desire.

The midrash on the parable (11:9–13) depicts the persistence of prayer in terms of action: ask, search, knock. Luke borrows these verses from the Q document, and they have a parallel at Matthew 7:1–11. Matthew features bread and stone, fish and serpent, good thing and good gifts, while Luke has fish and serpent, egg and scorpion, good gifts and the Holy Spirit. Since this passage comes in the series involving discipleship, one could petition only for those things deemed necessary to that discipleship.

Homiletic Commentary

In the sense that Luke's Jesus talks about prayer, it can never effectively be a "to whom it may concern" affair. One is not to fling out the random petition to the stars. As the gospels'

Jesus appeared to understand it, prayer began with an intimate address to "abba," father. For the Christian deist or agnostic, that makes prayer a difficult matter. If a would-be pray-er cannot conceive of an "abba" waiting with listening ear, his prayer may well die upon his lips.

That is when silence becomes one special friend and human initiative presents itself as the only option. The Benedictines say "ora et labora"—pray and work. For some Benedictines I have known, their work has become their prayer and vice versa. If there is no "abba" or if one cannot conceive of such, the only real-time alternative to prayer is work—working for what one might otherwise pray for. With Aquinas' observation on the legitimacy of prayer in mind, one could say that it is legitimate to work for that which it is legitimate to desire.

FINDING SOCIAL JUSTICE
IN A CHRISTMAS TEXT

Luke 1:39–55

In the days of Herod's rule Mary hurried off to a town in the hills of Judea to the home of Zechariah where she greeted his wife, Elizabeth. Elizabeth was pregnant and when she heard Mary's call at the door, the child leapt in her womb. She was seized by the Holy Spirit and cried out, "Blessed are you among women, Mary, and blessed is the fruit of your womb. Why am I so fortunate that the mother of my Lord comes to visit me? And Mary replied, "My soul magnifies the Lord, and my spirit rejoices in God my Savior, for he has looked with favor on the low estate of his handmaiden. Certainly from here on all generations will call me blessed; for the Mighty One has done great things for me and his nature is holy. His mercy is for those who fear him down the generations. He has shown strength with his arm; he has scattered the proud in their own vain thoughts. He has brought down the powerful from their high places, and lifted up those at the bottom of the heap. He has given the hungry to eat, but turned away the wealthy from his table. . . ."

Rubric

The abiding figure of Mary, said to have been the mother of Jesus, is writ large at the beginning of Luke's gospel. The passage above follows immediately upon what is known as "the annunciation." In it Luke depicts a divine messenger known as Gabriel making a visit to Mary at her home in Nazareth to inform her that she is pregnant with a child destined to reclaim the Davidic throne and make it an eternal one.

It is enough to receive such a visitor, but the message conveyed is astonishing. She who is (in the Greek text at hand) not "virgin" (*parthenos*) but literally "one who has not been known by a man," is nevertheless with child. Luke apparently decided to avoid the semantic problem of Matthew 1:23 where the Greek *parthenos* ("virgin") is a dubious and perhaps tendentious translation of the Hebrew *almah* ("nubile woman of marriageable age"), which appears at Isaiah 7:14). On the other hand, the Septuagint was the text from which Matthew probably worked.

Such uncertainty has never prevented the purveyors of dogma from pronouncing the birth of Jesus a miracle accomplished without the inconvenience of sexual intercourse and thus identifying the deity as Jesus' father both in spirit and in truth.

It is worth noting that by the time "Luke" compiled the text of this gospel passage, nascent Christianity was in the process of moving beyond its contest with post-Temple Judaism and into more aggressive competition with the Graeco-Roman myth religions—and in particular, we must suppose, with the cult of the Caesars.

It remained for Suetonius in his Lives of the Caesars ("The Deified Augustus" 94:4) to report the assignation of the god Apollo with Atia, the human mother of Octavius (by his own later declaration, "Augustus"), resulting in the latter's miraculous birth and thus entitling him to be considered a god. While Suetonius's work appeared some 30 or more years after Luke and more than a century after the birth of Octavius, he (Suetonius) was undoubtedly pulling together strands of an oral tradition that included tales of Octavius' special birth.

The question is why Suetonius' story of the conception of Augustus is scoffed at as fantastical and consigned to mythology while millions of Christians do not bat an eye at Luke's story and take it literally. Of course, this kind of anomaly has furnished such journeymen scholars as I with work for lo these many years.

Workshop

Luke seems not to have considered how a 160-mile round trip, no doubt on foot, through rugged terrain, would have affected a pregnant young woman. For he has Mary undertake just such a trek from Nazareth of Galilee to an unnamed village in the Judean countryside. And less than a chapter from now he will have a terminally pregnant Mary and the cardboard figure known as Joseph travel 90 miles from Nazareth to Bethlehem in the same fashion.

The burden of this passage, however, is neither the itinerary nor the mileage, but the connection Luke creates between the foretelling of Jesus' birth and the actual birth of John the Baptist. Luke invents a kinship of sorts between Mary and Elizabeth, said here to be John's mother. Is this Luke's way of trying to tie together what probably came to be opposing traditions of their sons, including a motif of conflict that seems to have persisted as their posthumous followings competed for attention (see Acts 19:1–7)?

The story becomes melodramatic when in 1:41 Luke tells us that the fetus in Elizabeth's uterus leaped at the exact moment Mary announced her presence to Elizabeth. In the evangelist's imaginative scheme of things, the fetus evidently by then taking shape in Mary's uterus has no similar reaction to the presence of Elizabeth and her leaping fetus. Is this Luke's subtle and coded way of saying that the future Jesus would have nothing to fear about John eclipsing him, while the pre-natal John already knew the identity of Jesus as messiah and himself as a lesser figure?

Luke has Elizabeth marvel that the vessel of the messiah's journey should come to her (1:43), thus underscoring Luke's ranking of Jesus above John, but here not in opposition since they will be kinsmen even as their mothers are depicted as kinswomen. However, see Genesis 25:22, the only other scriptural instance of in-utero leaping—the twins Esau and Jacob depicted as "struggling together" in Rebekah's body, set against each other from the beginning.

Elizabeth continues with her praise (1:45) thus setting the stage for Mary's peroration known in the Christian tradition as "Magnificat." Whence the Magnificat: vv. 47–55? Its poetry is based in great part on the prayer of Hannah at 1 Samuel 2:1ff. Allusions to several Hebrew Bible texts are also obvious: Deuteronomy 10:21, 1 Samuel 1:11, Job 22:9 (a negative approach), Psalms 25:5, 99:11, 103:17, 107:9, 111:9, 113:5–6, and Micah 7:20.

The theology of the passage is as follows: The biblical god, by whatever name, is savior or is found in the saving person of messiah (v. 47). This is so, we are asked to believe, because of the divine intention to honor someone of the peasant class (vv. 48–49). Divine favor will be conferred on those who respect the divine bias for the lowly (v. 50). God deals otherwise with the high and mighty: the failing of their fortune is of divine initiative (vv. 51–52). God intervenes in the distribution of resources among rich and poor (vv. 53–54).

Homiletic Commentary

Where this text is concerned, those who own as a primary dictum of biblical religion the so-called virgin birth will miss the mark by so much that they will surpass their usual level of irrelevance. The Magnificat is the centerpiece of the text, the rest pretext.

The Magnificat is Luke's brief for mythical Israel against the world, for the poor against the rich. There are not two sides to this story. It illustrates what the author (following Matthew at 5:3–6) will have Jesus say at Luke 6:20–21: "Blessed are you poor, for yours is the kingdom (rule) of God. Blessed are you who are hungry now, for you will be filled. . . ."

There can be no mistaking the partisan nature of this passage and of its author(s) and editor(s). It is the original liberation theology derivative of the eighth-century BCE public intellectuals Amos ("Let justice roll down as waters . . .") and Micah ("to do justice, to love mercy"). That is why the enjoining of neighbor-to-neighbor love will be for Luke the doing of justice in the way his Samaritan outcast will minister tenderly to the one we must assume was in Luke's imagination one of the privileged Judean elite—all depicted in the famous passage at 10:30ff.

Christmas begins its infringement on the public consciousness no later than mid-October. When the day itself at last arrives, the world is weary of it and, except in the seasonal uptick in charitable giving—a phenomenon due more to Charles Dickens' "A Christmas Carol" than to the gospel—its celebrations mostly miss the point. Nevertheless, insofar as social, economic and political justice is concerned, the Magnificat says it all.

THE NON-ANXIOUS
PRESENCE

Mark 4:35–41

When it was evening, Jesus said to his close followers, "Let's go over to the other side of the lake. Leaving the crowd that had followed them, they ushered Jesus into their boat just as he was (i.e. with no particular preparation for a voyage). Other boats followed. A storm blew in and the waves nearly swamped the boat. Jesus was asleep on a cushion in the stern. They woke him up, saying, "Teacher, don't you care that we may all drown?" Awakened, he spoke to the waters saying, "Peace. Be still." Just then the wind died down to a dead calm. Jesus turned to them and said, "Why are you frightened? Have you yet no trust?" And they were awe-struck and said to one another, "Who is this guy that the wind and the sea do what he says?"

Rubric

In this passage, the disciples are first terror-stricken by a windstorm on the Sea (inland lake, really) of Galilee, and subsequently awe-struck that Jesus seemed to have shut down the storm with three words of one syllable each: "Peace! Be still!" Those who over time have done more sailing than puttering about in a dock race will likely know about such terror.

I experienced it myself once as part of a crew aboard a 22-foot E-scow in the middle of a lake that is 18 miles long, three miles wide and in some places nearly 300 feet deep. A

71

squall line crossed our course bringing with it winds close to 40 knots. That's when the stomach turns to jelly and primal fear exudes from every pore.

On that occasion the man at the tiller was a seasoned sailor who'd seen it all and knew how not to be caught broached to the wind. Outwardly unperturbed, he kept her bow tight into the wind, tacking only slightly to and fro until we reached leeward shelter not much the worse for wear.

Our skipper had spoken to neither wind nor water. In fact, he spoke to us—and sharply—telling us to cut out our nervous chatter and sit still to windward. Even after all these years I clearly recall that the skipper's crew that day was pretty awe-struck at his mastery of craft, weather, and water. He didn't make the storm go away, but he brought us to shore unharmed. And he did so as a non-anxious presence* with calm dispatch.

Workshop

Not to put too fine a point on it, but a clue in verse 35 presages the storm. It is said that Jesus wanted to "go to the other side." Awaiting him on the other side (see Mark 5:1–2, the passage immediately following this one) is the Gerasene demoniac, who for Mark represents disorder and chaos. The storm was chaos of its own, and Mark depicts Jesus making the wind behave in an orderly fashion—orderly, that is, for those who wished to use it as an engine of transportation. Yet why should not the wind be itself and blow at gale force?

In any event, Mark arranges for Jesus to remain on the other side long enough to deal with the demoniac's disorder, but only by transferring the agency of the poor man's personal chaos into a herd of swine, a catastrophe for the swineherds who would now have to explain to their employers, the owners of the swine, how it was that they had run headlong, lemming-like, over a cliff and into the sea and drowned. So much for hog futures. Jesus, Mark says, returned to whence he had come, being no longer welcome there: "Then they began to beg Jesus to leave their neighborhood" (5:17).

Several thoughts:

1. The "sea" or "great deep" in antiquity represented the place of death. It was over a great deep and its writhing that the Priestly writer of Genesis imagined the gods (elohim) brooding and from it wresting life. Did Mark see and make that connection with this story?

2. It is highly doubtful that any of the authors of the canonical gospels ever knew the person or persons behind the figure "Jesus of Nazareth." Thus do the depictions of their individual versions of that figure derive in some part from the versions of the stories each used to bolster his desired theological or ecclesiological agenda.

3. "The other side" may in part represent for Mark what he figured Jesus must have faced in his public career: a plethora of dead traditions the maintenance of which was often burdensome to the poor and disadvantaged (see, e.g., 2:27–28.) Even on his own side of the sea, he has already had to face down the Jewish establishment (in the form of a demoniac) in the Capernaum synagogue (1:21–28). "On the other side," both figuratively and literally, he is to encounter criticism, detraction, and finally death—the final act of the same chaos seen in the storm at sea and in the twisted countenance of "Legion."

4. It is that same chaos Mark will depict welling up in the women at Jesus' burial place (16:1–8), making them afraid and unable to tell anyone what they have seen and what they have not. No Pollyanna, Mark; he seems to have sensed that chaos was never far away. History had already proven him right. It keeps doing so over and over again.

5. A passage from Job (38:1ff) thematically connected to the gospel story offers another take on the "wind and

water" motif, suggesting that Yahweh can speak out of a whirlwind to insist that He is master of all the attendant phenomena and has "set bars and doors" against the trespass of the unwitting. Maybe Mark's Jesus, there in a boat nearly awash and on the verge of capsizing, was seen to speak with the same authority as Job's Yahweh. Personally, I appreciated the skill and determination (his authority, if you will) of the skipper who was at the tiller of the E-scow T-18 that day.

6. A minor note: Job 38:1 (NSRV) includes words that should be inscribed somewhere in every preacher's study, graven on every pulpit, and drilled into every clerical head: "Who is this that darkens counsel by words without knowledge?"

Homiletic Commentary

Let us for the purpose of this discussion stipulate that something like the event described in the Markan passage under consideration may have occurred. It would not have been unusual for those who were said to have begun their lives as fisherman to have access to a boat for use on that inland sea, roughly 16 miles in length and eight miles across at the widest. Let us say that the author of Mark was himself familiar with maritime enterprises—or at least knew some who were.

Let us further suppose that, at one time or another, a group of persons more or less united in their fealty to the liberal version of Judaism that Mark advanced in his gospel were together on a boat and were caught in a storm. Let us say that by one means or another they weathered it without disaster or injury.

We might imagine such a group of individuals, once ashore, rejoicing that that they had not perished and once the storm had passed could resume their journey. They may have compared that struggle, one reminder of which they were still wringing out of their wet garments, to their against-all-odds mission of passing on and living out the liberal version of Judaism the revered wisdom teacher of their movement had once articulated, e.g. "love your enemy," "forgive infinitely," "turn the other cheek" — passive resistance, in other words. (Just as Robert Frost said in the concluding line of his paean-in-verse to New Hampshire, "At present I am living in Vermont," so I must acknowledge that not one of the sayings referenced above appears anywhere in Mark.)

The disciples may have found that their experience with the storm at sea made a good metaphor for cheering on those whom they were trying to add to their ideological community.

Thus they might they have said something like this to potential recruits:

"We won't lie: We'll always be in the minority, and what we teach and try to exemplify will challenge society and cause us trouble just as it caused our founder trouble, even unto death.

"But we sense that he is with us still in the profound wisdom of his teaching. We are persuaded that his teaching, if practiced by enough people, can save the human race from itself. It is this conviction that sustains us through trouble. It is this trust that provides the calming effect we need to help us keep on keeping on."

We can only imagine that Mohandas Gandhi, Martin Luther King, Jr., and Nelson Mandela were sustained by the same calm.

Notes

*This term was coined by the late Rabbi Edwin Friedman.

IT MAY LOOK LIKE A
MIRACLE, BUT IT'S
A PIECE OF WORK

John 6:1–14

A large crowd was following Jesus from place to place because they were amazed at the works he was doing. He retreated to a hillside, and the people followed him there. The approach of Passover caused him to ask one of his followers, Philip by name, where they were going to buy food for the people to eat—though Jesus knew how he would handle the situation. Philip was incredulous, observing that 200 denarii—half a year's wages—wouldn't buy enough bread for that crowd. Andrew piped up saying that he had spotted a boy who had brought with him five loaves and a couple of fish, "though what is that among so many people?" Jesus, ignoring that point, told his disciples to have the people sit down, which they did, some 5,000 of them. He took the loaves and the fish, made the customary blessing over them and passed them out to all who were seated. He asked that any leftovers be saved, and when they were gathered up, it turned out that there were 12 baskets filled with them. The people interpreted what had happened as a sign, and said of Jesus that he was the prophet who was to come.

Rubric

With this passage from John—one of the five in the New Testament that speaks of what has come to be known as "the feeding of the five thousand"—we enter that difficult territory of trying to account rationally for what so many take as evidence that "miracles do happen." At the outset, let us remember that the English word "miracle" is often a translation of the Greek *ergon*, which means "work." [Other Greek words thus translated are "teras" (wonder) "sāmeion" (sign) and "dunamis" (power)]. In the Bible the word "work" means, in effect, the result of what one is supposed to do because of who he or she is. A wood worker (or common laborer) ("tektōn") is known for his woodworking or common work.

Workshop

When Jesus is depicted as having done something of an extraordinary nature, it is as often as not deemed a "work." John, the gospel writer, used the term to account for the healing of the lame man at 5:20. Then at 7:3 Jesus' disciples want him to go to Judea and show off his "works." At 10:38, the term is used again in a similar context. At 14:11, Jesus is depicted as telling Philip, who is confused about whom Jesus represents, that if he can't figure it out from what Jesus says then he should try looking what he does—i.e. the "works."

Thus can one say that in arranging for five thousand people to eat their fill from scarce resources, Jesus was "doing his work." That might suggest that the gospel writer, who could have used *teras* (wonder) or *sāmeion* (sign) rather than *ergon* (work) to label the event, meant to say of Jesus, "Well, that's what he does. It's his work. Big deal."

In John's account what did Jesus actually do? Not much. He received the five barley loaves and two fish contributed by a youth (perhaps under some pressure), made the blessing over them and passed the food around. The barley loaves would have resembled pieces of pita bread. You could break five of them into bite-sized bits and maybe 100 people could get one each, though of course that would not be (as the text says) "as much as they wanted."

Thus have generations of homilists supposed out loud that the youth set (or was caused to set) an example for others both by bringing food and sharing it, thus multiplying the available supplies sufficient unto the day.

What's missing from John's version of the mass feeding is the confrontation that Mark, Matthew, and Luke tell us occurred between Jesus and his disciples. In John's version, Jesus raises the issue of how the crowd that has followed him will be fed. In the synoptics, the disciples ask the question and suggest that Jesus send the crowd away to find food. "You give them something to eat," is Jesus' rejoinder.

The disciples, it is said, go among the people looking for food to confiscate for the greater good, and do, in fact, locate the famous loaves and fish. Mark, Matthew and Luke make no reference to the youth who appears in John's version of the story.

All four gospels remark on the leftovers—12 baskets full. What size the baskets were we do not know, but the point is made that from five loaves and two fish a great deal remained.

Homiletic Commentary

Are the 12 basketfuls the "work?" Or is the "work" the satisfied crowd? Or is the "work" whatever John or anyone imagines Jesus to have done? How one decides to answer those questions will determine what significance the text will have for him or her.

If the respondent decides to go with whatever Jesus said or did to feed the crowd, the choices are simple. Either Jesus had the power to turn five loaves and two fish into a meal for 5000 people, or he had what it took to get people to share what they had brought.

If it is the former, then Jesus had magical powers and could have made the five loaves and two fish feed 10,000 people, 100,000 people and so on and so on. The "work," then is what Jesus said or did. Old-school Catholics may think in this regard of what they used to hear at the holiest moment of the mass as the priest said over the bread: "Hoc est corpus meum," supposedly acting in the name of Christ to make plain old bread into the Bread of Life.

If it is the latter, one might suppose that Jesus possessed such a commanding presence or persuasiveness that he could convince people to do what might not necessarily come naturally to them: to share what they had—or, along the lines of Matthew 5:40/Luke 6:20, to give it up entirely. In that case the "work" is what the people did.

If the answer focuses on a crowd whose individual members have been adequately fed (Mark, Matthew and Luke make the point that the need for food was mentioned toward the end of the day when people would ordinarily take nourishment), then that in itself is the "work."

A central point often missed or overlooked in the teaching about this passage is that end result: hungry people were fed. It doesn't matter who gets the credit for making that happen, and it doesn't much matter how or by what agency the hungry were fed. It matters that they were fed.

In a world beset by widespread hunger, and in some places even out-and-out starvation, the focus might best be on the shrunken stomachs, the parched lips and the beseeching eyes of the malnourished. Getting something somehow to them in a form they can ingest and digest is the "work" to be done by those who can do it. Not surprisingly, those hungry who are fed may take that good fortune as a sign, a wonder or power. And we don't care. Those who make it happen will know that it is a "work" that had to be done.

As Mark, Matthew and Luke told the story, Jesus put the responsibility to feed the people upon his disciples. "You give them something to eat." That is the most powerful homiletic point of all.

One can see what might well have been the model for the crowd-feeding story in the gospels by citing a passage at 2nd Kings 4:42ff. A measured amount of barley and corn is brought as first fruits to Elisha, who instructs that it should be given directly to the people. The concern is that it won't be enough, but Elisha says that there will be some left over. The people ate, and there was.

ASTRONOMY AND ITINERANT MAGICIANS

Matthew 2:1–12

During the reign of Herod and after Jesus was born in Bethlehem, astrologer-magicians from the East came to Jerusalem, asking, "Where is the child born king of the Jews? We observed his star at its rising, and we have come to pay him homage." Herod heard about this and was frightened about it (anxious that his heirs not be deprived of the throne), and all of Jerusalem, too. He called together a council of the priests and scribes of the people and asked where Messiah was supposed to be born. "In Bethlehem in Judea," they replied, "as predicted by the prophet Micah." Herod made quiet inquiry about seeing the astrologer-magicians in person and subsequently learned from them when they had first seen the star of which they spoke. He asked them to locate the child and bring him word so he could also go to pay homage. The astrologer-magicians started out and set their course by the star until they found the place, whereupon they saw Mary and the child, knelt before him and presented him with the gifts they had brought: gold, frankincense and myrrh. And, having deduced that Herod was up to no good, did not return to him but went home another way.

Rubric

To what great lengths the author(s) of Matthew went shows in the merging of the Persian *magoi* (in the Greek:

one *magus*, two *magoi*) with the birth narrative of Jesus,
the incorporating of an actual astronomical phenomenon
with the reign of Herod, and throwing in messianic predic-
tions for good measure. Unwittingly, Matthew cursed the
modern American church with the annual bathrobe-and-
turban ritual as children depict the magi and their gifts in
pageants in every time zone. By way of his text, Matthew
also gave us one of the most popular Christmas carols set
in poetic line and memorable tune by John Henry Hopkins,
Jr. (1820–1891). The carol ("We three kings of orient are") is
actually for the Feast of the Epiphany, but it is nonetheless
used across the long Christmas season—from mid-October
to Christmas Day.

Our task in this essay is to de-mythologize the text and to
extract and distill its significance for our own time.

Workshop

Except for assistance from obscure allusions at Isaiah 60:6
and Psalm 72:10b–11, Matthew is entirely on his own with
the story of the "magoi from the East." Nothing in the other
synoptics or John in any way parallels this text. One sus-
pects the story serves a peculiar Matthean agendum, and it
might be the work Matthew set out for himself in the task
of including Gentiles in the emerging Jesus Judaism communities toward the end of the first century CE. Already in
1:1–16 and 18–25, Matthew has legitimized Jesus for Jews;
now he demonstrates that Jesus is accessible to Gentiles as
well.

"Magoi" were certainly not unknown in antiquity.
Herodotus identified both priests called magoi among
the Medes and their descendants as priests of Zoroaster.
The book of Daniel (see 1:20, 2:2) mentions magoi. They
were generally associated with pre-astronomy. So the type
would have been known outside of the communities out of
which Matthew's gospel emerged. In addition, Luke in Acts

8:9–13 writes of one Simon who "had previously practiced magic (*mageuōn*) in the city."

Modern astronomy accords a flicker of verisimilitude to Matthew's tale, for a triple conjunction of Jupiter, Saturn and Mars occurred in 7–6 BCE, at about the time the one or ones called "Jesus" would have been born, if the cross-referencing of dates in biblical and extra-biblical sources is correct. Herod died in 4 BCE, according to Josephus in *Antiquities*, Book 17, chaps. 6 and 9. We may assume that Matthew, writing around 80–85 CE, would have heard of what must have been an extraordinary celestial display less than 100 years before, and combined it with his and others' knowledge of Persian astrologers to create the story of the magoi and the Star of Bethlehem.

Matthew's placing of the words "king of the Jews" on the magoi's lips has an effect similar to his bold declaration in 1:1 and 18 that already Jesus was the Christ. How could Matthew imagine it would be credible to have the wandering magoi know that a star heralded the birth of a Jewish king? Was this an allusion to Numbers 24:17 ("There shall star from Jacob come forth, and a scepter from Israel rise up")?

Certainly Herod, a Roman puppet of Jewish blood, would not have been interested in competition from the people of the land, which is what the Jesuses we meet in the synoptic gospels would have been. Perhaps Matthew's story is a veiled way of saying that Rome had no puppet in Jesus as he would become in the movement of Jesus Judaism an icon of leadership, if not a king. Herod was also the great renovator of the Second Temple that, in the eyes of late first-century Jesus Jews, had been replaced by the "risen Christ."

Where Matthew goes from there, as the magoi are dispatched by a troubled Herod who meanwhile has found out from his priests about Micah's prophecy (5:2), is through three more dream sequences—each, as it were, a literary *deus ex machina*. The first and second serve to get Joseph, Mary, and Jesus into Egypt and, after Herod's death, out again; the aim is to fulfill, as Matthew would say, Hosea 11:1: "Out of Egypt have I called my son." The third is to get them to Galilee, possibly to fulfill Isaiah 11:1: "And a shoot shall come out from the stump of Jesse, and a branch shall grow out of his roots." It is interesting to note that the Hebrew word we translate "shoot" and "branch" is the probable root of "Nazareth," the name of a village in lower Galilee. The presentation of costly gifts as befits royalty may have been Matthew's way of saying to the Jews of his community that Gentiles may become adherents of Jesus Judaism, but it will cost them.

Homiletic Commentary

Matthew has created one of the most memorable stories in scripture. Although it was long ago co-opted for the celebration of Epiphany, its imagery is by common consent part of the Christmas tableau. Those who teach or preach this passage will want to treat it for what it is rather than what it is not. Matthew 2:1–12 is surely not an account of something that actually occurred. What we're dealing with here is an imaginative word-picture, almost a tone poem that conveys a sense of temporal and spatial expansiveness to the appearance of the Jesus figure.

Whoever the real Jesus was, if he was real, he would have been born just as any other human being is born. In first-century CE Galilee he would probably have been from peasant stock or just a cut below, if his father really was a "tektōn," i.e., a day laborer. It was the various reports about his early adult life that set him apart and caused messianic hopes to be assigned to him. Some believed he was not only the Anointed One (messiah) of Jewish expectation, but a figure of such universal import that celestial phenomena would cause alien priests to seek him out. All that's missing is a 100-piece symphony orchestra and Dolby wrap-around sound.

EVOLUTION: FROM VENGEANCE KILLING TO AN EYE FOR AN EYE TO TURN THE OTHER CHEEK

Matthew 5:38–42

Jesus said, "You know that it used to be said, 'An eye for an eye and a tooth for a tooth.' But I say do not resist. If someone hits you on your right cheek, turn the other to him, and if any one threatens to sue you to get your shirt, just give it to him along with your coat; and if someone forces you to go one mile, go the second voluntarily. You also have heard that you should love your neighbor but hate your enemy. Wrong. I'm telling you to love your enemies, for if you love people who love you, so what? Try to be mature instead of infantile. Don't be a Gentile. Be a Jew."

Rubric

This passage would appear to be the heart of the Jesus ethic by which human nature is most sorely tried and mostly found wanting. The ancient "eye for an eye" injunction seems on the face of it barbaric. But what appears to have been its original intent was to control the wreaking of vengeance, or as W. S. Gilbert would much later put it, "Let the punishment fit the crime." It is difficult from a civilized twenty-first-century perspective to accept that "an eye for an eye" once represented progress. But it did. Under that dispensation you would not be justified in killing your neighbor's wife and children and burning his house down if in some act of aggression he blinds one of your eyes. You are entitled only to blind one of his.

Workshop

It's called "evolution" when ideas as well as life forms adapt and by adaptation survive or promote survival. Human ethics have evolved from a cave-man kind of behavior pattern to the passive resistance of Mohandas Gandhi and Martin Luther King, Jr. in which retaliation of any kind is proscribed. What was once *geschrieben* is now neither adequate nor accepted. What is now accepted in the arena of human conduct is "turning the other cheek" to the smiter.

In the Mediterranean culture, striking another person's cheek with the back of the left hand was a well-known and established major insult. Basic human instinct and the maintenance of honor and dignity would seem to demand striking back. According to the Jesus ethic, the victim passively asserts that dignity and honor by presenting the other cheek, daring the attacker to strike again. The idea is to make the aggressor think twice about what he has done and not to start a war.

The demand for one's coat should be answered not by resistance but by peeling off one's shirt as well. This is not passivity but passive resistance. If it is true that the Jesus of the synoptic gospels was thought to have come out of peasantry, he would have known the thin line that exists between poverty and destitution. The coat-as-well-as-shirt move would go hand-in-hand with the "if-then" proposition later stated in Matthew at 16:25ff to the effect that loss of life is gain.

In a practice copied from the Persians, a Roman soldier or government official might order a Palestinian to carry his gear for one Roman mile (5,040 feet or about 80 yards less than an English mile). The Jesus ethic says the one thus ordered should do a second mile voluntarily. Why? For two possible reasons: 1) to maintain one's dignity and 2) to make a supposed enemy sufficiently curious about what would have seemed an odd piece of conduct to consider the human worth of the person so conducting himself.

"Give to anyone who asks," is the mandate. The assumption is that the one asking is in greater need than the one asked. This utterly countercultural instruction assumes a radically egalitarian state of affairs in which "from each according to his ability, to each according to his need" is the governing concept (see Acts 4:32–35).

The end of the passage calls on those who would heed the words attributed to Jesus to be "teleioi" as the deity is "teleios." "Perfect" is not a helpful translation. "Mature" or "rounded in character" in the sense of being "finished'" (as in finishing school) works better. The Hebrew version of this image can be found at Deuteronomy 18:13 where the injunction is to be "tamim"—that is, "complete" or "whole."

To attain such a mature or finished state will require—on top of turned cheeks, ceded coats and shirts, walked second miles, and giving liberally—the loving of one's enemy, that is, the same one who struck or sued or required the first mile of burden bearing. The "finished" or "mature" one will recognize a human being like himself or herself in every other human being and will treat him accordingly. Or as the Episcopal Church's baptismal liturgy has it, striving "for justice and peace among all people" and respecting "the dignity of every human being."[1]

Homiletic Commentary

The Jesus of whom the writer(s) known as Matthew wrote evidently believed that human beings had it within them to live by Hillel the Elder's summary of Torah: "What you hate do not do to another." In fact, at 7:21 Matthew has Jesus paraphrase that proposition in positive terms: "In every-thing do to others as you would have them do to you." That ethic was thought central to the idea that "the kingdom of God is within you." It is not a *quid pro quo* kind of thing like "I'll love you if you'll love me." It is an unconditional "I love you because you are you."

On the face of it the mandate seems to ask the well-nigh impossible of human beings who are, after all, human. But it seems clear that Jesus' ethical corpus offers a different version of "being human." Being human or "only human" does not necessarily mean being less than the ideal as a matter of course. It can mean being truly human. Of that we are presumably capable.

That idea flies in the face of theology all the way from Paul to Augustine to Karl Barth and beyond. Paul scoffed at the idea that human wisdom could be of any avail. But that is not what Matthew's Jesus seemed to be saying. He is credited with the idea that the kingdom or rule of heaven is within the person or within the covenanted community, meaning that "salvation" has little or nothing to do with some other time or condition, but rather with the here and now.

The ethical wisdom inherent in the verses of this Matthean passage is, if not "the" key, at least "a" key to human sur-vival on the planet, to the vision of not only enduring but prevailing.

Notes

1. *Book of Common Prayer 1979*, p. 305.

THE CHRISTIAN GOSPEL
IN 15 VERSES

Matthew 25:31–46

When humanity[1] emerges in its complete self, all the nations will be arrayed before it and will be separated as sheep are separated from goats. Those who attained humanity will be on the right. Those whose behavior was less than human will be on the left. Those on the right will find themselves enjoying the fullness of the rule that their lives helped fulfill. Those on the left will be out of luck. Why? Because when one of us was hungry, you fed him; when he was thirsty you gave him something to drink; when he was excluded as a stranger you included him, making him welcome; when he had no clothing, you clothed him; when he was sick, you took care of him; when he was imprisoned, you visited him in prison. Those on the right will at first wonder when they did any of that, but then will come to see that in doing it to another they did it to themselves. Those on the left will have to acknowledge that they did none of those things, and in not doing them to another did not behave as human beings. Thus they will never understand that "eternal life" means the joy of knowing fulfilled potential. They will be, as it were, on the outside looking in—and, like as not, aware that they did it to themselves.

Rubric

If the Gospel according to Matthew were a collection of symphonic works, the passage above would be comparable to Beethoven's Ninth Symphony, the crowning glory of it all. Matthew begins a crescendo toward his Ninth with the parable of the wedding banquet at 22:1ff. The themes progress: willingness, readiness, preparedness, timeliness—all relate to the *parousia*, or the imminent future that is about to become present along with judgment (as in testing the strength or validity of a thing). Outer darkness, the home of weeping and gnashing of teeth, is to be the sure fate of one tested and found wanting.

The passage at hand is often called a parable of the last judgment. It may be more a parable of an ongoing judgment in the sense of a means-to-an-end evaluation. Its glory is its devotion to the ethical base of Jesus Judaism and to what, both in the end and all along the way, is important. It is not doctrine; it is not dogma; it is not right cultic practice. It is a prescription for human behavior.

Workshop

The sense of the passage reminds one of the succinct ethic enunciated in James 1:27: "Religion that is pure and undefiled is this: to visit orphans and widows in their affliction. . . ." One is tempted to rationalize the judgment aspect in the passage by saying that the reward of doing good is in its doing—in other words, consequential. Human experience validates such a rationalization. Matthew insists that not doing good, i.e., failing to attend to the needs of other human beings, is punishable by eternal damnation. Jews and Christians are more accustomed to "thou shalt nots," than to "thou shalt not fail to." It is a rude surprise. Sins of omission turn out to be as bad as those of commission.

It is an amazing scene Matthew paints, and in intense color and texture. It is global in scope and universal in its sweep. Before "the Son of Man" (or humanity at its best)[1] will stand assembled the individuals of the race. They have come together to receive their due, which may be more than consequential. It may be punitive in nature. They are separated (perhaps self-separated) Matthew says, as sheep are separated from goats: those who will inherit the rule or kingdom and those who will not. And what shall be the deciding factor? Personal accomplishment? No. Honors? No. Accumulated wealth and position? No. Being inoffensively "nice"? No.

The separating factor will be what each did for the good of other human beings. Those who did good will be heirs. Those who did not will go down the chute to *kolasin aiōnion*, eternal punishment. They will not have behaved toward the hungry, the thirsty, the lonely and ill-fed as human decency would demand.

From the late first-century CE perspective, this passage would have to be considered admonitory and cautionary. What it represents is solid evidence that the Jesus Judaism then emerging into the Christian church was fundamentally an ethical religion with far less emphasis on dogmatic and ritual aspects than later practice would suggest. It partakes in the same essential humanism as Luke's definitive parable of the Good Samaritan and of Dives and Lazarus (see Luke 10:29–42 and 16:19–31).

Homiletic Commentary

The parable of the sheep and the goats has all the effect of a minor key finale to a crashing and somewhat dissonant symphony, the final resolution of which will lie somewhere beyond the score and in the lives of those who have heard it and perhaps have been moved by it. Its effect is stunning and fearsome. Its challenge is robust, but does not present an impossible hill to climb. It asks only that human beings look at the weakest and most vulnerable among them as bosom brothers and sisters, and reach out to them in love and care, doing so as a learned, if not natural, response to obvious need or suffering.

Matthew 25:31–46 is the gospel in fifteen verses. It's all there. You could base a religion on it and never be the poorer for it.

Notes

1. "Humanity" is a possible translation of the Greek idiomatic phrase *huios tou anthrōpou*, elsewhere often rendered as "the son of man" or "the One like us."

ASSETS AND LIABILITIES — AND HOW TO KNOW THE DIFFERENCE

Luke 12:13–21

Someone in the crowd said to Jesus, "Teacher, tell my brother to divide the family inheritance with me." Jesus replied, "Who made me judge of this kind of thing? Be careful about greed, because your life does not consist in a lot of possessions." Then Jesus told them this parable: "A wealthy man's land produced an abundant crop. And he wondered how he would find a place to store it all. He hit upon the idea of pulling down his old barns to build larger ones wherein to store all that he had grown. He thought of himself as most fortunate, with nothing to do but relax, eat, drink, and enjoy himself. 'Soul,' he said to himself, 'You've got it made.' But God said to him, 'You're a fool, mister. You will die this very night, and all this you have now will belong to whom? Not you. You should have been storing up a different kind of treasure.'"

Rubric

One guesses that those who first heard this parable could scarcely grasp the context, because it seems fairly clear that the Jesus imagined to have told it, like most of his audience, came from peasant stock and knew wealth only in the abstract. If that surmise is true, then we need to ask what was the idea of trying to teach those with little a lesson about those with much. The answer may be that wealth is a relative matter, that what one does with what one has, however much or little, is of lesser importance than what one is and does with his finite life.

Workshop

On the occasion depicted in this passage Jesus is mistaken for a village sage—one of those whose job it was to adjudicate disputes and act as a kind of rabbinical, small-claims court judge. The dispute is over a brother's inheritance and another brother's claim to a share of it. Is the latter a younger brother, who, like the prodigal of Luke chapter 15, would have been entitled to a smaller share than an older brother? Has the elder brother claimed the entirety of the estate? Luke doesn't seem to care, because the point of the story is that material wealth is in itself irrelevant.

In a parallel text in the Gospel of Thomas (72), Jesus turns to his disciples, asking them, "I am not a divider, am I?" Probably a rhetorical, palms-up, shoulders-shrugged question. Just behind Jesus' reluctance to get involved in a dispute between two brothers is the reluctance to get drawn into a feud about money, a subject that seems not to have been a priority for Luke's Jesus.

Luke, the master storyteller, does not allow the wealthy landowner of the parable to think for one second of distributing some of his bumper crops to the poor and needy, or of sharing it with other landowners whose crops had not been so plentiful.

Luke wanted to portray him as a fat cat with money in the bank. Luke even makes him refer to himself as *psuchā*, the New Testament word "soul," meaning the comprehensive and essential self. But the self-satisfied landowner was in fact reacting only with part of himself—the part that sees only self in the single dimension of a mirror and therefore at only one moment in the grand sweep of time and circumstance.

Thus it is not soul talking to soul, but one dismembered part talking to another. In our time, it's called "compartmentalization," as if such a thing were actually possible apart from neurotic denial. Living life in small, discrete, disparate parts is not really living.

It is somewhat unusual in parables for the divine self to be assigned a speaking role as in verse 20; perhaps this is an indication of how deeply Luke felt about the unequal distribution of wealth: "Fool! Tonight they take your soul (whole self) from you." What an image! In the darkness of a first-century night illuminated only by firelight or moonlight (if either) the very essence, the all of the rich one would be exacted from him, leaving him a husk—not unlike an empty barn! Luke depicts the deity speaking directly to the man, "Who will own all this that you have gone to such ends to amass?" It is a rhetorical question, of course, to which the answer is, "Anybody but you."

Here the glum wisdom of Ecclesiastes fits: "It is an unhappy business that God has given to human beings to be busy with . . . I hated my toil in which I had toiled under the sun, seeing that I must leave it to those who come after me—and who knows whether they will be wise or foolish? Yet they will be master of all for which I toiled. . . ."

Homiletic Commentary

In the gospel's own counterintuitive way, we learn that barns bursting at the seams, treasuries overflowing with money, and safe deposit boxes stuffed with securities are liabilities, not assets—unless thought is given to using them to relieve the needs of others.

This passage and its parable offer rich possibilities for the preacher with the courage to confront a congregation with the clear demands of the gospel where material resources are concerned. This is true of middle-class congregations in the United States—even or especially in a time of economic constriction and uncertainty.

How this lection might be preached in a sub-Saharan mission is, of course, another thing. But in the venues where most readers of this analysis craft or consume sermons, the implications are obvious. Large treasuries and fat endowments upon the interest of which congregations are willing to live are a perversion of the gospel.

The Christian church sometimes resembles a gated community within which life goes on in unruffled security, regardless of what is going on outside the gate. Inside the gate theological orthodoxy and ritual correctness become paramount issues. And as those are parsed, ample time remains for the anathematizing of churches and church leaders who dare, for example, to admit of human equality for gay, lesbian, bi-sexual and transsexual persons.

The loudest praise for one particular parish minister I know was that "he built up a big savings account for us, and now we have no worries." Wanna bet?

THE ONCE-BLIND
NOW SAW

Mark 10:46–52

As Jesus and his disciples were entering Jericho, a large crowd was leaving. Bartimaeus, a blind mendicant, was sitting by the road. When he heard that it was Jesus of Nazareth who was coming, he shouted out, "Jesus, Son of David, have mercy on me!" People in the crowd told him to be quiet, but he persisted in shouting louder, "Son of David, have mercy on me!" Jesus apparently heard him and stopped dead in his tracks, saying, "Call that man here." And they did, saying, "Take heart, man, get up. He wants you." So throwing off his outer garment, he jumped up and went directly to Jesus. Jesus said, "Well, what can I do for you?" The blind one said, "Rabbouni, let me see again." Jesus replied, "Go; your trust [in me] has made you well." Immediately, Bartimaeus regained his sight and followed Jesus on the way.

Rubric

"I can't see," can mean a lot of different things. To a patron in a theater it can mean that a tall person or some one wearing a large hat has taken the seat just ahead and the view of the stage or screen has been blocked. To a person in a room in which all the lights have just gone out, it means that he or she is temporarily blinded as the pupils adjust. To one who cannot find his glasses when asked to read a document, it means that until he finds them he will be unable to see enough to read. When you add "it" to the end of "I can't see," it can mean that a person, asked to confirm or agree with another's observation or conclusion, says "I can't see it," meaning that whatever the other sees is not plain to him. "I turn a blind eye to it," says a person who prefers not to admit cognizance of one thing or another.

Sight is one of the five elements that make up a human being's sensory equipment. Being deprived of it at birth or later due to accident or disease is a serious disability that can be only partly compensated for, and then only by courage and diligence.

The ability to perceive an image, a sound, a taste, a smell, or a touch is part of what it means to be fully human. Those who lack one or more of those means of perception are markedly disadvantaged, though such heroic figures as Helen Keller and Ludwig van Beethoven found impressive and noble ways around their disabilities.

A real difficulty is that many people with all five senses intact still cannot "see" or "hear" or otherwise perceive a truth that is as close to them as their own skin. At Mark 4:12 we encounter this paradox: "Seeing they may see and not perceive; hearing they may hear and not understand" (see also Isaiah 6:9–10).

It will be helpful to have all that in mind as the above reading from Mark is considered.

Workshop

By 10:46, Mark's narrative has placed Jesus and his disciples in Jericho, from whence they are leaving for Jerusalem. (Matthew agrees with this itinerary [see Matthew 20:29ff], but Luke [see Luke 18:35–43] places the incident during Jesus' approach to Jericho.) In any case, the apostolic company was located about 12 miles northeast of Jerusalem and drawing ever closer. On the way out of Jericho, Mark's narrative says, there was an encounter between Jesus and a "blind mendicant" or beggar. Mark gave him a name: "the son of Timaeus" or Bar-Timaeus. C. S. Mann and other commentators would like us to take the naming as a sign of the story's authenticity, arguing that assigning a specific name to such a man represents an actual person in an actual historical event.

What is to be made of the name and the naming? Remembering that Mark was compiling his narrative in a community of Jesus Judaism post-70 CE, one might wonder what would have been the point of giving the blind mendicant a Greek name: Timaeus, and then adding the Semitic prefix "bar" (son)? Is it to indicate that he was a Gentile convert to a transitional Judaism? That may be the significance of the words given Bartimaeus to speak: "Jesus, Son of David."

The more important point is that the blind mendicant is depicted as having known in some way about Jesus and that Jesus might have been able to help him. Not a bad way to witness to the egalitarian impulse not only of Jesus as he may have been (and as his ethical teachings reveal him to have been), but of what Mark may have hoped his community would become. A blind beggar would have been pretty far down in the ranks of first-century CE Palestinian society. His affliction would have marked him as a sinner, and his poverty would have further marginalized him in a vicious social cycle. That helps us understand why Mark had Jesus ignore the "many" who told Bartimaeus to be quiet (10:48).

Mark's Jesus was on his way but allowed himself to be deterred. He forthwith dealt with the person who had called after him. The upshot is well known. The son of Timaeus, whoever he was, received his sight because of his audacity — and, as Jesus is said to have said, his trust. If sight is synonymous with life, then perhaps the restoration of Bartimaeus' sight represented for Mark what the "raising of Lazarus" represented for John (see John 11:1–44). In each case, it was a last great act of a powerful agent before he confronted an establishment that feared such power.

Homiletic Commentary

"Restraint" is the word that should immediately come to mind as the homilist sits down to prepare his or her pulpit commentary on this passage. The text and its placement in the narrative are so rich with possibilities that it may be tempting to overreach.

One point often overlooked by homileticians is that the so-called "healing" was the result of a serendipitous conjunction of need and resource. In Mark's imagination, Bartimaeus "saw" his one chance to change his life and forced a meeting with one he somehow thought could effect that change. He was audacious and believed that such a change was possible. Any way you look at it, the story is one of a huge, last-gasp bet on the remote possibility of a huge transformation—a bet that paid off.

When the story is told that way, it suggests that Bartimaeus was the agent of his own healing, a notion that finds support in Mark 5:34, Matthew 9:29, and Luke 8:48. If that proposition can be considered, then a homily or study session on this text could explore what Mark meant by depicting Jesus as a more or less passive player in the drama. He is said to have done nothing but have Bartimaeus come front-and-center and then tell him that by doing so he was able to "see." What can Mark have imagined about that encounter that might make it so powerful, and how can it be replicated so that those who see but do not perceive might at last come to perceive? What kind of strategies does that suggest to churches whose members want to stop doing what they've always done and being what they've always been so they might see what it is that will actually attract people who want and need a Bartimaeus-like transformation of their lives?

TAKING SIDES

Mark 12:38–44

As he was teaching, Jesus said, "Beware the scribes, who like to walk around in long robes and to be addressed with honorifics in the marketplaces, and to have the best seats in the synagogue and places of honor at formal dinners. What they do in fact is to take widows' houses from them, but for the sake of appearances say long prayers. They will receive the greatest condemnation." Jesus was seated across from the treasury, and watched the crowd put their money in the receptacles. Many rich people put in large amounts. A poor widow came and put in two small copper coins, which are worth a penny apiece. He called his disciples to him and said, "Indeed, I tell you that this poor widow has put in way more than all those others. They have contributed out of their abundance; she out of her poverty has given everything she had."

Rubric

I would be invited to teach neither in a Shiite masjid nor in a Lubavitcher synagogue, much less in any evangelical church. My teaching, considered heretical by many Christians, would be an outrage in those venues. The Jerusalem temple, in which Jesus is depicted by Mark as "teaching" (διδαχη), was a symbol of all that Mark's Jesus was protesting against. The text must mean that he was holding forth somewhere in the vast outermost court, the total circumference of the outer wall being nearly a mile.

One supposes he may have attracted a few like himself, dissenters from the temple's business as usual.

In fact, he warned those whom he was teaching to "beware of"—that is, keep your eye on—the scribes, the traditional Jewish teachers with whom he differed on many issues including presumably what they were teaching, but whom he here criticized only for their public behavior. To an objective observer it could have sounded like jealousy. The scribes got the nice vestments and the best seats in the house, all the while robbing widows—read here "powerless women." No doubt on whose side Mark's Jesus was.

The challenge to the readers of According to Mark in any age is to take sides with the poor, the dispossessed and those looked down upon by the religious pooh-bahs. Has anything much changed where the latter are concerned? The clergy get the splendid vestments and the seats up front and most of the air time in public worship. Beware of them.

Workshop

As far as we can tell, this passage is comprised of two distinct sections (in academe they are called "pericopes") with the common thread being the image of the widow. First there are the scribes who allegedly "take widows' houses from them" (probably "appropriate" or "foreclose on" is how we would put it). Second is the poor widow herself who puts into the temple treasury (receptacles resembling large trumpet bells) two small coins λεπτα δυό, a rich gift in view of her poverty. Worse yet, it stood in tragic contrast to the large sums that the scribes were pocketing from the sale of the humble dwellings of other widows—women with no right of inheritance and powerless before the world.

What of the much-maligned scribe—the Greek word looks like "grammarian" but means something more like "stenographer"—he who is ridiculed and defamed through-out the gospels? By the early part of the first century CE, the scribe had become a combination bureaucrat-academician in the tradition of the post-exilic elder Ezra. Scribes tended to be laser-beam focused on Torah, the source of their power and privilege. In Mark's eyes, the interpretation the scribes applied to Torah was cramped and narrow. He also saw them as liturgical bloviators (12:40b).

Whether or not any of this was true of scribes generally rather than only some of them (the "few-rotten-apples-in-every-barrel" theory) is hard to know at this remove. What is certain, however, is that Mark's narrative is part of his continuing assault on the religious establishment as he knew it to exist just as the middle third of the first century CE gave way to the last third. The implication is that Mark's Jesus took the same dim view as he did. That would have put Jesus on a collision course with the establishment, just as Mark, followed in due course by Matthew, Luke, and John, would go on to narrate.

One notes a remote connection between the Mark reading and that portion of 1 Kings 17 concerning a widow of Zarephath who is spared starvation by a jar of meal and a cruse of oil that seem never to run out. A visiting prophet did not devour the widow's house, but shared it and her food with her—perhaps an egalitarian act that could be contrasted with the scribes' elitist behavior.

Homiletic Commentary

Many years ago I was faced with a major life decision. I had to decide whether or not the only kind of congregation worth my time and energy was a large and prominent one. I would not say I was required to spend a great deal of time researching the decision, because it soon became apparent that those clergy who were chosen to lead large congre-gations had generally restrained whatever avant-garde impulses they might have had so as to appear to be of one mind with the majorities in those congregations. And those majorities invariably slouched toward the conservative end of the spectrum. Once incumbent, those leaders tended to stay within the bounds of the middle course to avoid offending overmuch the factions at either end.

That amounted to what I took to be the very thing St. John the Divine was fretting about when he wrote the words, "Because you are lukewarm, and neither hot nor cold, I am about to spit you out of my mouth" (Revelation 3:16). Not disposed by nature to be lukewarm, I had to take what seemed to me the intellectually and ethically honest path. I tried for a time to walk about the temple porticos in rich vesture and to preach the middle way, but in the end I could not do it.

I had become pastor of a particular Detroit congregation just a year after the ruinous 1967 street rebellion some called a "riot." It changed everything, mostly for the worst. It revealed for all to see the deep and abiding white racism of a city's treatment of its African American citizens. It revealed a level of poverty and hopelessness that had trapped hundreds of thousands in a ghetto circumscribed by invisible boundaries but defined by what the Kerner Report had described as separate and unequal opportunities.

I knew that the religious communities of the city had to respond as they had responded at the height of the rebellion when the city was on fire. Now that the fires were out, systemic changes needed to be made, and made quickly. So I said as much in sermon after sermon, declaring that it was no longer possible for the church to go on with business as usual, parsing the old texts and re-running the same old routines.

All too many of the city's residents were like the poor widow in the Markan text: struggling to make ends meet while a bloodless economic system was devouring what

little they had, even as they strove to meet their basic re-
sponsibilities. I said that, too, and made more enemies than
friends. I guess I expected it: I had Mark to back me up.

EVIL WITHIN
AND WITHOUT

Luke 8:26–39

Jesus and his friends arrived by boat in the country of the Gerasenes. He was no more out of the boat than a man from there who had been possessed by demons for a long time came near him. The man wore no clothing and he lived not in a house but among the graves in the local cemetery. When the man saw Jesus, he fell to the ground in front of him and shouted at the top of his voice, "What do you want with me, Jesus, you who are Son of the Most High God? I beg you, do not torture me." Jesus had already ordered the unclean spirit out of him. Jesus asked him what his name was. He answered, "Legion," meaning that more than one demon had seized him. In fact, the demons begged Jesus not to send them into the abyss, the place of the dead. Nearby was a herd of pigs feeding on a hillside, and the demons implored Jesus to let them seize the pigs. Jesus said yes, whereupon the pigs threw themselves down the hill into the lake and drowned. When the keepers of the pigs saw this, they ran away and told about it everywhere, causing people to come to the hillside to see for themselves. When they arrived they saw the formerly possessed man sitting with Jesus, They asked him to leave the area because they were afraid. Jesus obliged and got into the boat to leave. The man from whom the demons had departed earnestly begged to go along, but Jesus told him to stay were he was and tell his story there. And so he did.

Rubric

The slogan "Jesus is the answer," or some variation upon it, shows up on bumper stickers, outdoor church signs, and across the intellectual flatlands of fundamentalist Christianity. The slogan generally means that Jesus is the answer to everything and to anything. The observant Jew, practicing Muslim, or secular humanist would dissent from that baseless generalization, for all of them would find such a claim to be not only without warrant but also downright silly.

Though none of the canonical gospels makes that claim overtly, they do so in more nuanced ways. Luke 8:22–25, 26–39, 40–48 and 49–56 basically set forth that claim, since Jesus is said to have calmed a storm at sea by the mere speaking of a word, to have cured a man's insanity by driving the demons out of him and into a herd of swine, to have passively cured a woman's hemorrhage without being aware of the action, and to have called a child back from the dead. Just an ordinary day in the life of a savior, I guess. No wonder an uncritical reader of the bible could come to conclusion that "Jesus is the answer." No wonder also that nineteenth- and early twentieth-century hymn writers of evangelical Protestantism would descend to such doggerel as this to express their raw and unrationalized faith:

> I was sinking deep in sin, far from the peaceful shore
> Very deeply stained within, Sinking to rise no more,
> But the Master of the sea heard my despair cry,
> From the waters lifted me, now safe am I.
>
> James Rowe, 1911

Workshop

Much of Luke chapter 8 feeds the belief that Jesus is the cure-all. The passage immediately preceding the one at hand in this proper begins a series of several so-called miracle stories that were clearly intended to bolster the image of Jesus as a doer of extraordinary, even supernatural deeds. Luke 8:22–25, the story of his command to a stormy sea to subside, was meant to show Jesus' mastery of such natural phenomena as wind and waves. Luke places the word *epistata* (master) on the lips of the frightened disciples as the inland lake known as the Sea of Galilee kicks up a storm that threatens to capsize their little vessel.

Once the storm is banished and the boat comes ashore, another storm, so to speak, shows up in the person (or persons) of a madman from whose chaotic madness Jesus will be depicted as wresting control. One may be put in mind of the image struck at Genesis 1:2 in which the gods (elohim) are said to have "moved over 'the formless void'" (in the Hebrew idiom "*tohu va bohu*," meaning something like our idiomatic "helter skelter") and wrought from it the beginning of order.

Now with the apostolic company back on dry land comes the possessed man who had been living in the local cemetery ("among the tombs"). He was naked and no doubt wild-eyed. It is said that no mesh of chains could restrain him when the demon exerted itself over and within him. Having taken over the distressed man's larynx, the demon Jesus had exorcised is depicted as crying out: "What have you to do with me, Jesus, Son of the Most High God?" Luke makes an interesting point without actually saying so: even if the average sane person doesn't get who Jesus is, the powers of evil recognize him at a glance.

At v. 30, Luke has Jesus ask the creature, "What is your name?" (*onoma*). The word can also mean "character" or "nature." That's how the demon takes it, for the answer is: *legiōn*, a Latin word remade into Greek, meaning in practice "six thousand" as a Roman legion numbered 6,000 soldiers. In case we do not understand, Luke adds, "for many demons had entered him."

Luke depicts the demons as beseeching the exorcist not to send them "back into the abyss." Here the Greek is *abussos*, indicating the dwelling place of the dead with their warden Satan. It is interesting that *abussos* is the word the Septuagint uses to translate the Hebrew *tehom*, the "deep" of Genesis 1:2. Tehom is the rough equivalent of Tiamat, the monster of chaos in the Babylonian creation myth. The herd of swine is substituted for chaos.

Luke's story is 1) that the swine are driven by the demons into the sea—shades of Exodus 14:27–28; 2) that the people are generally frightened by what they have seen; and 3) the demon-less man wants to join up with Jesus but is told to go home and tell everyone what happened to him.

Homiletic Commentary

Among the homiletic opportunities this passage presents, I would emphasize two: 1) an exploration of what it meant that Luke did not depict Jesus as simply destroying the demons—that the narrative did not allow him to send them into the abyss for good, and why some practitioner of animal husbandry was the financial victim of the exorcism; and 2) a creative commentary on why the exorcised, who would have provided great PR for Jesus, was told to stay home and tell his story there.

As to the first, it is an interesting worldview that Luke's disposition of the demons represents. In contemporary terms it could be said that evil, as such, is not easily brushed away, that it is ever-present in the evolving world, and that the abyss is never as far away as we think. Even a cursory review of the horror of the Nazis' near-annihilation of European Jewry requires a look directly into that abyss. The growing xenophobia in America with regard to gay and lesbian persons, Hispanic immigrants in the Southwest, and the obvious Tea Party hatred of Barack Obama are foul emanations of that vile stink hole.

As to the second: One does not need ordination or a commission to go to a far land to preach the gospel. One does best to grow where he or she is planted and to do the good thing right there. For example, if you live in Arizona, you might join Episcopal Bishop Kirk Smith in his denunciation of that state's recent Nazi-esque immigration law. That would be an exorcism well worth doing.

Since we began with a Sunday school hymn, we may as well end with one:

> Brighten the corner where you are;
> Brighten the corner where you are;
> Someone far from harbor you may guide across the bar.
> Brighten the corner where you are.

> Ina Duley Ogden, 1913

FED TO
THE WOLVES

Luke 10:1–11, 16–20

The Lord [as Jesus was known in nascent Christian communities toward the end of the first century] appointed 70 others and sent them on ahead of him in pairs to every place he intended himself to go. He told them, "The harvest is plentiful, but the laborers are few. Therefore ask the Lord of the harvest to send out more laborers for the harvest. Now look, I am sending you out like lambs into the middle of a wolf pack. Here are your instructions: Carry no wallet, no rucksack, no extra pair of sandals, and don't get hung up with people on the road. Whatever house you go into, first say, 'Shalom to this house.' And if anyone there answers your greeting, your shalom will be upon that person, but if not it will come back to you. Stay at that house eating and drinking whatever is set before you, for the worker deserves his compensation. Don't move about from house to house. As you move along, and people in a town welcome you, be attentive to the sick there and inform them that the rule of God has come near to them in their restored health. But anytime you come to a town in which you are not welcome, tell the people there that you are shaking the dust of the streets off your sandals as a protest of their inhospitality. Tell them that what will happen to them is worse than happened to the people of Sodom and Gomorrah. . . ." The

70 returned in joy and reported that even demons had submitted to them. Jesus told them he knew that because he had seen "Satan fall from heaven like a bolt of lightning. See how I have given you the power to tread with impunity upon snakes and scorpions and over the enemy; nothing will hurt you. But don't get too excited about all that. Just be joyful that your names are written in the place where Yahweh dwells."

Rubric

You could call it "lambs to the slaughter." Luke's Jesus used a similar allusion to describe his sending out of the 70 missioners as an advance team: "like lambs into the midst of wolves." Such an idea would be incredible to those engaged in animal husbandry in any age. The herdsmen's job is to keep predators away from the flock, and especially the more vulnerable lambs. Those Luke imagined being sent ahead by Jesus were, in military terms, the first wave. Those in the first wave of a landing or an invasion usually sustain high and heavy casualties—as would lambs if they were driven into a wilderness of wolves, perhaps to sate the wolves and spare the sheep that would come later.

Among the possible echoes of this are contemporary jihadi, perhaps even suicide bombers. Did the author or authors of According to Luke remember accounts of Roman persecution of Jews and others who got in the Empire's way? Or did they know of actual resistance with which early Jesus Jews had to contend? And was the idea to sanctify the pursuit of a lost cause? Until one gets to the end of the passage, which seems highly optimistic in nature, one does not know that the lambs were not eaten by the wolves—or if they were, the struggle was worth it because the names of the "70 others" are "written in heaven." It has a tincture of the "70 sloe-eyed virgins-in-paradise" promise: one virgin per missioner.

Workshop

In these verses from Luke 10 with their report of the commissioning of the 70 (or 72, the confusion stemming from the Hebrew and the Greek Septuagint's rendering of the number of "nations"), we may be getting a glimpse of the late first-century church's modus operandi. The significance is that the "70 others" who are sent to the "nations" are an expansion of the commission of the 12 to exert authority over demons and the diseased (9:1). The question we would like to ask is what Luke meant by writing first of the 12 and then of the 70. Perhaps it is a reference to the author's (or authors') intention to write "an orderly account" (1:3). The order of things that Luke depicts began with Jesus and his initial community called "the 12," obviously a literary nod to the 12 tribes of Israel. A later generation with an expanded apostolate is represented by the 70.

The marching orders for the 70 in chapter 10 differ from those of the 12 in chapter 9. The 70 are sent as innocent and vulnerable lambs into the teeth of the wolf pack. If Paula Fredriksen is right about Galilee in the first third of the first century CE being relatively free of onerous Roman presence, especially taxation,[1] maybe the original first-century communities did not experience the same degree of trouble as those toward the end of that century, to which dangers Luke refers in his lambs-to-the-wolves analogy.

Compounding their natural vulnerability (as lambs into the midst of wolves), the 70 are to "carry no purse, no bag and no (extra pair) of sandals" (10:4). The 12 were to have taken nothing at all: no staff (symbol of intrepid self-sufficiency—think here of Gandalf), no bread, no money

(9:3). Both the 12 and the 70 are told to shake off the dust of inhospitable venues from their feet in protest.

The 70 are to eat with the people they visit, cure the sick, and proclaim that, ipso facto, the rule of God has come as close as it was going to get. Nothing is mentioned about eating in chapter 9's commission of the 12. Its mention in chapter 10's commissioning of the 70 may reflect the custom of the fellowship meal. Eating together has a curative power all of its own as intimacy overcomes distrust. In his parallel account (his chapters 9 and 10), Matthew mentions food, but only in connection with just compensation for the worker—"the laborer is worthy of his hire."

Luke affords an interesting take on Mediterranean hospitality in chapter 10. In our modern Western understanding of hospitality, it is the host who has the advantage. The host welcomes whom he or she will. The sense of 10:10–11 is that the invitee gets to decide whether or not he is welcome and if the hospitality is sincere. And he may leave, shaking the dust of the place off his feet, leaving the host with the dust of his own habitation in his nostrils and egg on his face. Thus the unencumbered, penniless, purse-less, bag-less, bread-less, traveling-light itinerant will take his gift of freedom—with its potential to cure the sickness of too-muchness—to another threshold, hearth, and table.

Luke alone tells the story of the 70 going out. Luke alone writes of the success of that apostolic ministry, perhaps as a preview of Acts, "the second book." The 70 are depicted as returning in triumph "over the demons" (those human dispositions that conspire against hospitality—along with the peace and at least momentary social equity it nurtures—and that retard the return of wholeness).

The power "to tread with impunity upon snakes . . ." must be stiff-upper-lip cheerleading, because late first-century Jesus communities were regularly bitten by the serpents and scorpions of persecution. Members of the communities were hurt, reports to the contrary notwithstanding. That may be whence the idea that their "names are written in heaven."

Homiletic Commentary

Evidently Luke could not resist incorporation of the Q material of 10:12–16 (see the Matthew parallel at his 11:21–23) with its Sodom and Gomorrah-like curse. Luke 10:16 makes clear the bias of the gospel—namely, that Jesus and his derivative communities represent that deity whose rule the itinerant missioners convey by their very presence. If they are not "received" (as Matthew puts it) or "heard" (as Luke says), the non-receivers and/or the non-hearers have rejected life.

Here the homilist or student needs to be careful not to turn the proposition into Christian take-it-or-leave-it imperialism. Rejecting Jesus and his teachings as the early church worked them out does not make a person or a people evil. However, not treating the other as one wishes oneself to be treated can and usually does have consequences that range from inconvenience to catastrophe.

The wolves that kill and eat the vulnerable in our contemporary society include 1) an obscene disparity of wealth that leaves the few with abundance and the many with scarcity, 2) an airy disregard of those at the margins by those close enough to the center to know economic security and 3) a warped set of social values that weaves a web of sufficiency around the fortunate to the exclusion of the unfortunate.

Those persons, movements, and institutions that put aside concern for their own safety and comfort and enter the fray against such malign forces are the descendants of the 12 and the 70.

Notes

1. *From Jesus to Christ* (2d ed.; Yale University Press, 2000), p. xix.

WHAT MATTERS AND
WHAT WILL ENDURE

Luke 12:32–40

Jesus said to his disciples, "Do not be afraid, little flock, for it is your Father's joy to confer his rule upon you that you may observe and teach it. Here's how you will do that: sell what you own and give the proceeds to the poor. Make for yourself wallets that will not wear out in order to carry the unfailing treasure of that rule—which, because it is immaterial, no thief will be interested in stealing and no moth in eating. If you bury that treasure, you will for all intents and purposes bury yourself. Meanwhile, keep your work clothes handy and have your lamps ready to light—as would those waiting for their master to return from the wedding supper so that they may open the door for him when he knocks. The slave who is ready is a happy slave, for he will be served as if he were not a slave. It's like this: you have to be ready for anything because The One Like Us* is coming when you least expect it.

Rubric

It may be true that time, often said to be "of the essence," is in fact just that. Such is the leitmotif of the passage above. It mocks the notion that religion is a static thing, that one can come and go from its observance or study and find it just as it was when one's attention was diverted elsewhere. The trouble is that most appreciation of religion treats it as an antique worthy of preservation only in some pristine or mint condition.

This is not to suggest that the religion we find emerging from the gospels is apocalyptic in nature, or that the fundamentalists' rapture is just around the corner and that we should all decamp to the mountain top to await transport. It is merely to say that the way of thinking found in the gospels is dynamic in nature, always appreciating and seeking to understand as much of the present as possible, and attentive to the truth that what one does or does not do today is certain to have consequences for either good or ill tomorrow. A psalmist said it this way: "Teach us to number our days that we may get a heart of wisdom" (Psalm 90:12).

Workshop

It is no settled community to which this passage speaks or in which it may well have had its origins. This community is concerned not about what has happened or even what is happening, but rather what is about to happen. The attitude and deportment mandated are appropriate to a time and condition that is temporary. The traditional and customary rules do not apply. Material possessions are now only incidental to the main purpose of life, which it to be ready for the arrival of a new dispensation.

This probably reflects a real urgency that was felt in some quarters of late first-century Jesus Judaism to the effect that something would occur almost any time to resolve the chord set up by whatever happened to the Jesus figure and the resultant confusion of the community that had gathered around his countercultural teaching.

The passage begins with Luke's singular assurance that the "little flock" need not fear, because a new rule or dispensation based on that teaching will be conferred on them. How, is not clear, but it is safe to say the dispensation will have something to do with the idea first enunciated by Hillel the Great to the effect that the rule of life spelled out in excruciating detail in Torah and further excruciatingly parsed in Mishnah and Talmud centers on how one treats another. If one does not do to another what one hates or would hate to have done to himself, a community would experience less cause for fear. Or as the epistoler John will later write of that ethic, "There is no fear in love, but perfected love casts out fear" (1 John 4:18a).

One aspect of that ethic is illustrated by the counsel Luke gives his Jesus to speak: he exhorts the divestment of possessions in order to be able, through liquidation, to give alms. One sure thing about this is that it bespeaks a culture of freedom. To be liberated from the conservation and maintenance of much wealth would be to enjoy the rule that it has been the Father's pleasure to confer. Yet it is not as if the community is not to be rich. The community is to be rich in a way that is not liable to the erosion of time (moth and rust). Its treasure is not to be sequestered for the sake of compound interest, but to be shared by way of love.

This is because a time of crisis is upon the Jesus communities. As the first century drew to a close, they experienced both a longing for resolution and fear of what might befall their little minorities. The advice of Luke's Jesus in that situation is to be ready for anything at any time, keeping the work clothes at hand and the lamps ready to kindle. This means that "now" is the time, not "then."

This passage is saying that in every moment, in every face, in every event and development, there exists the potential for the new dispensation to emerge in its fullness. The community will not then wish to be encumbered by many possessions and concern for its security. When "the master comes" must be a time when the community is ready individually and corporately to enter wholeheartedly the new dispensation.

Homiletic Commentary

Among the homiletic opportunities in this passage is the proposition that the church needs to find ways to divest itself of institutional burdens that keep it from being effective as a herald and practitioner of the new dispensation. The church's heart will be wherever its treasure is, whether invested in attention to administrative minutiae, or in quarrels over matters of authority, or sunk in stocks and bonds, or in excess bricks and mortar—or in real work among real people with real needs.

If the church could discover, claim, and know the truth about its *raison d'etre*, it would be free to be what the gospel envisions and maybe what its Galilean hero may actually have been: that is, an embodiment of humanity at its best, existing to bid love and care for people rather than for things that are subject to the depredations of moth and rust and in the long run will not matter.

Notes

*A possible translation of "Son of Man."

A TOPSY-TURVY
GOSPEL

Luke 14:1, 7–14

On one occasion when Jesus went to the house of a leader of the Pharisee party for the Shabbat meal, he was being watched closely. He was watching also, and saw how other guests chose places of honor. So he told them this parable: "When you are invited by someone to a wedding banquet, do not sit yourself down in a place of honor lest someone more distinguished than you has been invited, and the host who invited both of you may come to you and say, 'Give place to this person,' and then in disgrace you would have to get back in line and take the lowest place. But if you went to the lowest place first, the host might come to you and say 'Move up higher,' and then you would appear as honored among the other people at the table, (proving that) those who exalt themselves are bound to be humbled while those who humble themselves have nowhere to go but up." He said also to the host, "When you give a luncheon or a dinner, do not invite your friends or relatives or wealthy neighbors, lest they invite you in return, thus repaying your hospitality. When you put on this kind of thing, invite the poor, the crippled, the lame and the sightless. They cannot repay you, but for that very reason you will be blessed in the resurrection of the righteous."

Rubric

Emily Post and Ann Landers would probably have agreed with the advice to play humble at a dinner party in hopes that you would be seated by the host somewhere above rather than below the salt. But each would wonder at the other piece of advice: don't invite the well-off who can return the favor; invite those who for obvious reasons couldn't. Life in the Hamptons, on Park Avenue, and Rittenhouse Square, in the leafy suburbs of the Grosse Pointes and Bloomfield Hills, on suburban Chicago's North Shore and elsewhere among the grandees of society would never be the same again if that counsel were to be heeded.

Thus in this passage we revisit the lines from Luke chapter 1 and the Magnificat: "He hath put down the mighty from their seats and hath exalted the humble and meek," and in the revisitation of them are reminded that the gospels' social analysis is largely egalitarian.

Workshop

Since we have before us an entirely Lukan passage with no observable parallels in Q or Mark, we are able to ask what particular agenda item in Luke's greater scheme these nine verses were meant to serve. Table hospitality in the Mediterranean world was serious business, highly symbolic, and every bit as well orchestrated as among the contemporary upper classes. In fact, Luke located several of his important episodes at the dinner table (see 5:29ff, 7:36ff, 11:37ff, 22:14ff and 24:30ff).

We are told that people were watching Jesus very closely as he approached his host's table. If like me you are of humble origins, and have been at a dining occasion well above your social station, you know how it is to have all eyes critically on you as you nervously ponder the array of cutlery in front of you and wonder which implement to pick up and when.

While Jesus was being checked out (and this event is not included in the appointed reading), a person with dropsy, which is characterized by large, unsightly swellings, appears. One wonders how a person thus afflicted could have gained admission to such an event. (Perhaps in the same way "the woman of the city who was a sinner" got into that other party.) As Luke depicts him on other occasions, Jesus was quickly diverted by the suffering man, but not so quickly as to miss an opportunity to take on the lawyers and Pharisees present: he asks them whether it is lawful to cure people on Shabbat.

No answer was forthcoming. In Luke's imagination their silence may have been a result of being flabbergasted by Jesus' effrontery, or of knowing the moral answer was different than the legal one. And so in their embarrassment and unwillingness to speak heresy they remained mute.

Not content to offend over the soup course, Luke's Jesus proceeds to assail the guests (and host!) over the entrée. He has unsolicited advice for both. To the guest: don't seat yourself too high at the table, because it's an assumption perhaps unwarranted by social conditions and it makes the climber liable to embarrassment if and when he or she is re-seated in a lower place. In short, the guest who came not to dine but to preen should play Uriah Heep and conspicuously take a lesser chair in hopes that such a gesture would bring social advancement.

It is a tad worrisome that the parable could well be taken as a lesson in social climbing strategy rather than as a mockery of such society games when the Who's Who concerns pale beside the specter of human suffering.

Now on to the host in question and to other who may soon be hosts themselves: Don't make up your guest lists from the social directory. Need and resource must converge. Moreover, those who have been marginalized unfairly must be brought to the center, not because they're among the 400 but because they are human beings who happen to be in great need.

Homiletic Commentary

Pity the parson with the country club just up the lane from the church. If the sermon is to be based on the gospel at hand, he or she must now go into the pulpit bearing a radically egalitarian message. Or he or she could take to text Genesis 27:11 KJV and avoid the issue altogether. Should the rector tackle the gospel in an intellectually responsible way, the next dinner party at the rectory had better include an habitué of the soup kitchen down in the city as well as the CEO of a big corporation who pays the largest pledge in the parish. In fact, the two should be seated together, the former just above the invisible line on which the saltcellar sits and the latter just below it.

"Jesus Christ!" exclaimed a clergy colleague who read this manuscript in draft and found himself aghast at the prospect of such a thing. "Exactly," was my reply, "Jesus Christ."

ABOUT THE AUTHOR

H arry T. Cook is a graduate of Albion College, Albion, Michigan, and of Garrett-Evangelical Theological Seminary at Northwestern University with honors in Hebrew. He is the author of *Christianity Beyond Creeds* (1997), *Sermons of a Devoted Heretic* (1999), *Seven Sayings of Jesus* (2001), *Findings: Exegetical Essays on the Gospel Lections* (2003) and *Asking: Inquirers in Conversation* (2010). He also wrote a biographical essay for *Life of Courage: Sherwin Wine and Humanistic Judaism* (2003). Recently retired after 42 years of active ministry in the Episcopal Church, he covered religion and wrote a weekly column on ethics and public policy for the *Detroit Free Press* in the 1980s and '90s.

9 781598 150292

LaVergne, TN USA
22 February 2011

217401LV00(